Face Forward

Meeting Challenges Head On in Times of Trouble

Michele Howe Clarke

NEW YORK

Face Forward

Meeting Challenges Head On in Times of Trouble

by *Michele Howe Clarke*

Disclaimer: The Publisher and the Author make no representations or warranties with respect to the accuracy or completeness of the contents of this work and specifically disclaim all warranties, including without limitation warranties of fitness for a particular purpose. No warranty may be created or extended by sales or promotional materials. The advice and strategies contained herein may not be suitable for every situation. This work is sold with the understanding that the Publisher is not engaged in rendering legal, accounting, or other professional services. If professional assistance is required, the services of a competent professional person should be sought. Neither the Publisher nor the Author shall be liable for damages arising herefrom. The fact that an organization or website is referred to in this work as a citation and/or a potential source of further information does not mean that the Author or the Publisher endorses the information the organization or website may provide or recommendations it may make. Further, readers should be aware that internet websites listed in this work may have changed or disappeared between when this work was written and when it is read.

Please remember that all memoir is based on memory; therefore, this story reflects what I remember to be true about events and people. Certain names, locations and identifying characteristics have been changed, and some individuals in this story are composites of more than one person. Dialogue and events have been recreated from memory, and, in some cases, have been compressed to convey the substance of what was said or what occurred.

ISBN 978-1-60037-960-4 Paperback
ISBN 978-1-60037-961-1 eBook
Library of Congress Control Number: 2011922430

Published by:
MORGAN JAMES PUBLISHING
The Entrepreneurial Publisher
5 Penn Plaza, 23rd Floor
New York City, New York 10001
(212) 655-5470 Office
(516) 908-4496 Fax
www.MorganJamesPublishing.com

Interior Design by:
Bonnie Bushman
bbushman@bresnan.net

In an effort to support local communities, raise awareness and funds, Morgan James Publishing donates one percent of all book sales for the life of each book to Habitat for Humanity.
Get involved today, visit
www.HelpHabitatForHumanity.org.

To my husband Dwayne who is my love and my trusted ally, my mother Esme who taught me to love myself, and my father Sidney who showed me the way forward.

Table of Contents

Part II: 21 Insights to Thriving — The 3 Principles of Prosperity....161

Through the Principle of Perception you will

Through the Principle of Preference you will learn to

Through the Principle of Power you will learn

Foreword

Stop. Right now. Stop for just one moment. Your life is about to change. Your thinking will be altered forever, if you are willing.

These pages are inviting you to stop and realize what really matters. To stop and see how good you actually have it. To stop and consider what you really want to do with your life. You will be reminded to tell those you love that you love them. You will appreciate things you normally take for granted. You will have a new perspective on your life. Maybe... for a moment, if you choose.

See, it's human nature to forget how good we have it. It's human nature to complain about our lives whether in whispers to ourselves, or publically at the top of our lungs. It's human nature to get caught up in the details of life while we miss the glory that is all around us. Then one day, if calamity strikes, our world as we know it comes screeching to a halt.

Michele Howe Clarke's world stopped with the breathtaking news she had cancer. She writes, "My mortal innocence stolen, I was no longer invincible." As she comes to terms with her mortality, she reaches out her hand and invites us along. With grace, humor and perspective, she shares her humanity and exemplifies the true meaning of courage. Real courage is all of it – feeling the fear, rage, devastation and horror and continuing on anyway. Through the darkness of her journey, she learns to see the beauty of life. Each time she glances in the mirror or catches someone staring at her disfigured face, she is forced to face what she has lost. As she masterfully tells her tale, we realize, she is speaking to us. When we know she has chosen to commit to living – not just surviving, but actually thriving, we can breathe a sigh of relief for her – and we are then faced with the choice to look at our own lives.

Michele has walked through what most of us can barely imagine. Just when it seems like it can't get any worse another dreadful trial emerges to derail her once full and successful life.

However, Michele has transformed her calamity into a zest for life coupled with a desire to serve the world. She takes on the issue of our cultural vanity with a vengeance. She is rigorous with herself, yet gentle with us. As her physical wounds slowly and painfully heal, she in turn peels back the layers of what she once held so precious, beginning with her smile and continuing deeper to her soul. She bravely confesses her over-reliance on her beauty as a way to connect and be liked. Yet, through the loss of her glorious smile, she discovers something more – she discovers what she is really made of and what has actually been there all along.

Our challenge is not to remain a spectator as we read. I challenge you! Allow this story to impact you. Allow your heart to be opened. Allow it to refresh your spirit.

Michele kindly softens the blow for us. She knows we might distance ourselves from her pain, which may very well cause us to miss this gift. She graciously gives us time to reflect as we read by providing sections where we can stop and consider. Speaking directly to our heart, she offers profound teachings such as dealing powerfully with our own personal turning points; seeing our self-defeating habits as a "Ponzi Scheme"; as well as advice on how to deal with our ever-chattering ego.

To further support us, Clarke has also designed 21 powerful insights for us to thrive.

Will we take her message, teaching and wisdom to heart? Will we actually allow another's trauma, struggle and triumph to enrich our lives? Maybe. It will take something. Predictably, we will put this book down, walk back into our lives and forget. Gradually, the effect may subside. We will go on with our days, our schedules, and our plans. We will get angry at the traffic, or the weather, or our spouse, or the dog. And, we will forget that for a moment we remembered what really matters.

May we never be faced with a life-threatening diagnosis or be left with physical disfigurement. Yet perhaps, in this moment, we will stop and take Michele Howe Clarke's wise words to heart. Right now, we could commit to wake up, to live the life we are here to live and to make the difference we are here to make. We could love ourselves as we are, accept our pain and our struggles and we could begin to "Face Forward".

Kristen Moeller, MS
Bestselling author, *Waiting for Jack: Confessions of a Self-Help Junkie— How to Stop Waiting and Start Living Your Life*

Prologue

It is said the only constant in life is change. A*in't life a bitch*? You can be trucking along just fine, thinking everything is peachy keen and BAM, life socks you a good one. The rug you have been standing on gets pulled right out from under you. As you fall ungraciously on your ass, you realize all was not as it seemed. The image you have been projecting about your life story has been shattered by an extraordinary event.

For me, my shattering event was head and neck cancer. It caught me mid-stride in a neat and tidy materialistic life. My story is that of a life abruptly changed: of a journey through hell and back. I am a woman greatly enhanced by a shattering life experience. For me there is no going back. I wear the scar of this battle on my face. I am marked forever. I can never forget. I am reminded every time I look in the mirror. My every interaction with others is impacted.

When I turned 33, I was 40 days into living with head and neck cancer. The right side of my face drooped down: slack and paralyzed. My reality was distorted. The appearance of my savaged face was shocking. I was on a rollercoaster of operations: three head-and-neck surgeries in 31 days with 18 of those days spent in the hospital recovering from being sliced open. The wound ran from the crown of my head to the middle of my throat. My right facial nerves were cut out from deep within the facial muscle.

My 'right' face now sagged. It was sacrificed for my chance to live. If that were not traumatic enough, add in a crazy infection. Green puss oozed from holes that formed on the side of my head, well, my ear actually. From the common observer's point of view, it would look like I had two ear holes on one side. *Nature can be so freaky.* I am told these are unexpected and rare complications with very low probability. *Hey, that's my style.*

This extreme period in my life was filled with raw emotion and, crushing realities. It was set in the backdrop of sterile halls and alien doctor-speak. I did the only thing I could—I began really living my life, enjoying the challenge, letting myself feel the pain. I learned to live through hurt and live in the present. I gave myself the time and space I needed to become better. I weathered the storms living through the bitterness and staying in process.

Cancer, and my subsequent disfigurement, showed me how enmeshed my life was in the Myth of Perfection. The Myth of Perfection is what I call the reality we live in today, especially in the United States. The Myth goes like this: I believed that if I looked good, had a nice body and clothes, owned my own home and car, had expensive possessions, I would be perceived by others as doing well; therefore, I *was* doing well. I was a vice president investment banker at one of the world's largest banks. I almost had the Myth in the palm of my hand, though I constantly felt perfection slipping through my fingers.

I had a smile that stopped traffic and gave people a reason to smile back. My smile was my passport into friendship and accomplishment. Many a time it had carried me through as nothing else could. I relied on and lived by my smile. Ironically that was the very thing I would lose. My mask was taken from me. There was nothing left to hide behind. All the imperfection that I secreted away now stood out for the world to see.

With a paralyzed face my imperfection was brought to the forefront, a fact that few missed. It has been incredibly difficult to be stared at, sometimes open mouthed, and whispered about behind cupped hands. It pierced my heart each time a child innocently mimicked my twisted mouth. It destroyed the Myth that I was living in: I could no longer ever be viewed as perfect.

My new face took away my ability to be egotistical. It ripped at the narcissistic, materially driven woman I had spent many years becoming, and thrust her into a world of spirit, healing and intent. I was gifted with an abrupt ending so that I could begin again from scratch. I shed layers of wasted self like the skin of an onion being peeled away. If I wanted a future I had to control my thoughts, today and everyday.

My tragedy and transcendent sacrifice could have easily led me to self-righteousness and indignation, even outright anger. Sometimes, many times, I felt all these emotions and more. Thankfully, the road to self-pity was not the path that inspired me. When all this was taken away, I believed a new beginning had to be found. I turned inward to discover that I was the source of all things. With my purpose rediscovered I began to Face Forward.

With a purpose and a desire for a bright tomorrow you can live with grace and enthusiasm. Walk with me on this very personal journey, I will show you my wounds. I will share with you my instrumental learning. You will be challenged to stand in your power and step into your brilliance. As you realize that now is the only time that matters you will begin to trust that what you need will be there when you need it. Through active choice you trust that your life, like the tiny acorn, came programmed with everything you need to become a strong oak. You learn to grow whatever makes you smile. You decide to reach for relief. You can feel your way to your best future. You become positively present and actively involved in mastering the power of your focus.

I am so excited for you to experience your amazing value and worth. You will learn to allow your greatness. You will lay the groundwork for your highest and best life, as you get out of your own way. You can own your authenticity and express yourself with confident intentions. You ask for what you want and dream weave it into your life. Begin to receive and believe what you need to masterfully create your life.

Part I

THE STORY

We all have a story we tell ourselves. Here's mine.

Innocence Lost

The tide has turned
My life is new

I was holding my six-month-old daughter, Sage, in my arms. We were looking out our Long Island City, NY, window at the Pulaski Bridge going from LIC, Queens to Green Point, Brooklyn. It was early spring and the sky was just getting dark. I dialed my sister, Nikki in DC. I talked to her on the phone regularly and to me it was just another quick chat before a minor surgery to laugh at how "of course, I, Michele, would have a benign growth behind her right ear and need surgery."

"So what exactly are they doing again tomorrow?" Nikki asked.

"They are going to remove the benign tumor in my parotid gland. Though it is head and neck surgery, they say it's fairly routine. There's a risk that they may knick a nerve and my face may become paralyzed. I should be up and about in a week or so, " I replied, sounding mildly exasperated by the whole inconvenience. I really did not want to have surgery. I wanted to put the whole thing behind me.

"They have to warn you about these things. It's like when I had Lasik surgery, I had to sign something that said I might go blind," Nikki added, picking up on my casual approach to my upcoming surgery.

"Yeah, I'm not really worried. The doctors have assured me there's nothing to worry about," I said.

"Good. You know you should take at least two weeks off. I think you could really use the time away from work. Are things any better?"

"No, more of the same. I'm still working crazy hours most of the time. I can't believe the stress I deal with for money!?" I mused.

"Yeah, the almighty dollar," Nikki retorted. "Sometimes I think that I could never go through what you do. Then I hear about the money you make and I can't imagine what that must be like. People would think you're mad to even think about leaving."

"Yeah, the yearly bonuses are heady stuff," I sighed.

"Well, I better get back to work, but have Dwayne call me when you're out of surgery to let me know all is well."

"Chant up some good vibes for me, sis."

"Got you covered, Miche. I always chant for you."

"I know, you're the best. Man, I can't wait for this to be history."

"You got this, Miche."

"Yeah, true that. I will ask Dwayne to call you. Talk to you soon; love you."

Sometimes it's in these everyday moments, that the surviving traces of life can be found; the end flash where everything was still normal, safe, and cozy. You were still in the zone where you had resided so comfortably. An instant, that if you could, you would warn yourself: *Hey, baby, brace yourself, here comes the heavy hitter.*

In Through The Out Door

I am going in
Everyone else is going out
What the hell is going on?

I had a hard time sleeping the night before the operation. Man, only I would have some rare growth growing behind my ear. I have always been one to get the weird and wacky ailments. When I was in college I had to have my tonsils removed, at 21! The doctors said it was atypical to remove the tonsils of someone that age.

At the age of 16 in a mad dash to find my permit so I could take my driver's test, I completely removed the second drawer of my desk with the intention of turning it over on my bed. I pivoted toward the bed, drawer in hand only to cut my leg wide open on the protruding runner of the drawer. I'll never forget looking down at my leg expecting to see a scratch, only to find that I had sliced my leg wide open: over an inch deep and about 5 inches long. I stared mesmerized by the white fat cells filling with red-hot blood. I remember being impressed by the thickness of the blood and how quickly it began to spill over my leg and onto the carpet. I grabbed my leg and cried out softly for my sister Nicole.

"Ni cc coo holl," I cried in a small broken voice. Then I called again this time just a little louder, "Nicoohol!" I was afraid that if anyone else saw the cut I might have to go to the hospital and delay passing my driver's test. That was NOT acceptable to my sweet -16 -year -old mind.

When the blood started falling and vividly staining the carpet I knew the jig was up; I had to get to Dad and quick. I held up my leg and hopped down the hall leaving a trail of blood as I went downstairs. My Dad took me to the hospital where we got star treatment because he was an attending physician there. 150 stitches later I had a lifetime scar.

My next adventure leading me to the ER happened when I was 17. The senior prom was just weeks away. I felt amazing - so full of potential, life was so sweet, it was nearly bursting. I thought of myself as a free spirit, a beautiful anomaly. I loved to party and was one of a mish-mashed posse who partied hard. We traveled in a pack of 20 to 25, more guys than girls. We had all run together for the last two years of high school.

Class had let out early that day. It was late in April. The sun was shining brightly and the sky was crystal blue. I had taken to riding my mountain bike the three miles to school since the winter weather had broken. I was looking forward to riding out that day, feeling the wind against my skin and blowing through my hair.

I slipped on my headphones and turned up the volume on my Walkman. The Cult's *Electric* blaring in my ears, the music's pounding rhythm propelled me quickly on the route home. I was excited about taking the jump I did daily. Usually I would take it at an angle and get about 4 feet of air for about two seconds. It was exhilarating and I loved the feeling of fear turning to adrenalin pulsing through my veins. That day I decided as my feet pushed the peddles in increasing speed that I would take the jump head on and fly through the air. I was sure I would get at least six feet of air and maybe coast in the air for even longer.

The jump was on the slope of a highway overpass. It was 20 feet up from the highest point. Just as I crested the top of it, I knew I was going faster than I had ever taken the leap before. The whole maneuver consisted of jumping a curb going over the sidewalk and over the gravel hill down to a parking lot below.

As I took the shot head on, I knew immediately it was a mistake. The ground was moving towards me at an accelerated rate. Instead of soaring out and forward in a gentle airborne flight, I was facing the ground head on. My bike was perpendicular to the ground. Then it happened: all at once I hit the ground. Or did the ground hit me? My front tire struck first, jarring the bike so hard that the brakes locked.

The next thing I knew I was crashing. My fall seemed frozen in time and space. I saw the handle bar meeting my eye; a bike spoke stuck into my chin just as I began eating gravel. Then the world went black.

When I came to a little while later, I thought, *"Hey, this doesn't feel too bad."* Then I started to rise and felt the whole parking lot tilt underneath my feet. I could sense a hot wet sensation dripping down my chin. I looked at my hands. I was surprised to see that they were all cut up and shaking uncontrollably. It was when I tried to take a step that I knew I was pretty banged up. All at once people started running out of the shops. A martial arts teacher assisted me into his store. He said gently, "Let me call your parents."

He dialed my mom and handed me the phone. As soon as I heard her voice I broke down and started sobbing. The proprietor took the phone from me with a gentle hand and I heard him say, "I'm sorry to say that your daughter has been in a bad bicycle accident and she is in pretty banged up. You should come and pick her up as soon as you can."

That night after my visit to the emergency room, I was dismayed to see my reflection in the mirror. My eye was swollen shut. I had gravel burn all over and a deep cut where the bike spoke had stuck my chin. I spent the night making a T-shirt to wear to school the next day. The front of the shirt said, "Let me guess, you want to know what happened…" The back of the shirt had multiple choices:

A. "Got into the ring with Mike Tyson"
B. "Parachuted without a parachute"
C. "Trying out a new prom look"
D. "None of your @#$% business"

All the plans for senior prom had been laid. The prom was less than three weeks away. There would be seven couples in our super stretch limo.

We would trek into NYC to a club after the prom. Everyone was pumped. We spent the weekends trying to work on getting a base tan. They were all watching what they ate and trying to get a little more exercise. Now all I had to do was heal quickly. It was a good thing that I always did heal quickly. Even the doctors commented on how remarkably fast I recovered.

You can bet your ass I was in that super stretch limo, not a scar in sight, leading the charge to maximum partying. I have a picture of me on my senior prom night next to my Mom and Dad. I was totally buzzing already from the pre-cocktail bonanza. I was smiling like a diva all shining in the glow of youth, puffing out my chest like a peacock. My parents, on the other hand, looked tight-lipped and slightly dismayed. I was their youngest and the wild child. *Who knew?*

Come to think of it, I have quite the scarred up body. I do have more than the usual kid-incident scars. My trips to the hospital started at age three when I had a run-in with a spoon that ended up embedded in my upper forehead. I, being the youngest of four, was always trying to do what my older brother and sisters did. My brother Bradley saw me grab hold of a spoon and fork.

Brad, being all of three years older, knew that I was too young to play around with a spoon and fork. I might slip and hurt myself. He ran after me yelling, "Give me back that spoon and fork. You know what mom says about running with utensils." I thought it was some sort of game. I squealed and took off running. He was after me like a shot. "I said, give me that fork and spoon," he screamed in a frustrated voice.

I laughed. I ran up to Brad and presented him with the fork. But I was off again before Brad realized that he held only one of the two utensils he had demanded. He was after me in a flash. Now he was getting mad. "Michele, get back here right now or you'll be in big trouble!"

He was charging after me at full speed. Meanwhile, I was running around and around the foyer in a frenzy of exhilarated screams. The foyer had a table right in the middle. The periphery held a brick fireplace with a sharp cornered ledge. As Brad rounded the corner he reached out to grab me. Calamity was staring me in the face. I tripped over the table leg. I went flying, spoon first, into the corner of the fireplace.

Brad stood up shaken, calling nervously to me, "Hey Michele, get up. You're all right." I did not answer. I just moaned. He knelt over me and turned me over saying, "Michele, stop kidding around." He gasped at what he saw. "Oh my gosh, Michele! Mom! Mom!" Brad screamed as he ran full steam toward our mother's room, leaving me totally freaking out with blood streaming down my face and into my sobbing mouth.

"Mom, Miche fell on the fireplace and there's a spoon sticking out of her forehead." Brad and I both were crying now. I was sobbing as blood coursed down my face. When mom pulled the spoon out, the spoon made suction sound. The running blood looked like a never-ending waterfall flowing down my face and dripping from my chin.

I lucked out that time and did not need to get stitches, though they might have been a good idea as I live with a dime-sized scar on my forehead. That scar provided many an entertaining yarn at the bars. I have to laugh at my accident-prone self. Sometimes I think I have a love affair with the emergency room.

Harsh Reality

Help me to be gracefully wise
An amazing cosmic magician
Who is self-assured, source-inspired, joyous and grateful
Who will always learn everyday

I had been in the operating room for more than six hours. I awoke from my morphine stupor, dying of thirst and starving for my husband's loving eyes and reassuring smile. After what felt like eternity, Dwayne appeared. He did not look reassuring in the least. He approached the bed with trepidation. Then he looked into my eyes. His eyes were full of tears. I could tell he had been crying.

"How did it go?" I asked in a gruff voice.

"The tumor wasn't benign but malignant, Michele. You have cancer and the cancer has moved to your facial nerve." He sobbed as he laid his head on my lap.

I stared at him, numb and disbelieving. What was he talking about? I was only 32 years old and a new mom. He was telling me that I would now be fighting for my life?

In a fog of drugs and denial, I found myself being wheeled into my hospital room where my sister, Sydney, and brother Brad, awaited my arrival. We hugged and cried, all of us utterly shocked and distressed. The surgeon informed me of this devastating news in a callous tone as if he had forgotten how to go softly.

He arrived and sat at the end of my bed and gave my calf a quick impersonal squeeze. I felt like he just wanted to move onto the next patient, perhaps he had seen too much of cancer's devastation.

"Ms. Clarke, when we got into the surgical site it was clear that cancer was running throughout the area. When the tumor was biopsied it came back malignant. You have Adenoid Cystic Carcinoma of the Parotid gland. Not only was the tumor we knew about in your parotid bed malignant but the cancer has spread out of its original site into your facial nerve. The cancer is aggressively involved in all your facial nerve branches on the right side of your face.

"We do not know how far the cancer has traveled; it could go as far as your ear canal or even to your brain. We were not able to get all of it out; we were unprepared for what we found. The cancer has grown out of its original site in the salivary gland, and the facial nerve is massively involved There is a need for another operation in order to remove all the cancer. In order to live, you will have to sacrifice the facial nerve on your right side. From what I have seen, I do not believe there will be any nerve left to repair; therefore the right side of your face will be irreversibly paralyzed. "

Tears started coursing down my cheeks as he continued, "Your appearance will be very altered and with the paralysis your face will droop and you will likely drool. I have had some patients who chose death over having to live with a paralyzed face."

I froze in shock and said in a broken whisper, "Yes, but I have a six month-old daughter." He nodded and said, "This is a supreme sacrifice but let me say that this cancer is aggressive and is known to lie in wait for years only to come back in the brain or lungs."

"How long do I have?"

"It's hard to say. The statistics say we are looking at under five years," he said emotionlessly with no expression. He showed no humanity, like a programmed robot.

"What happens next?" I asked, feeling helpless. I was losing control.

"We schedule the operation to remove the tumor and facial nerve, followed by an intense course of radiation."

The first choice I had to make was whether to live or to die. I could be a pretty corpse or I could sacrifice my facial nerve for a chance to live. For me, there was really no choice but to go forward with the surgery.

I stayed in the hospital after this first operation for five days, heavy with the knowledge that the next operation would be to remove my facial nerve. At the time, I was too numb to really be affected by the experience; I just took it. I had a tube sewed into my skin near the joining of my ear, known as a shunt, which would drain the operated site. I had been sliced open, my ear had been reattached and I had more than fifty stitches down my neck. Those five days were a haze. I shared a room with a very sick elderly woman. I was being introduced to a world where I felt frequently that I was the youngest fighting such a serious disease.

Turning Point

So now you know, you've met your mortality on the road. You can die, not at some distant time in the future, when you are 100 years old with gray hair and a frail body but today, young, vibrant, and full of promise. It can happen and you know it. You look around at everyone who doesn't and it brings a bitter sting and harsh questioning: WHY? Why me? Why now?

Continued on next page…

...continued from previous page

Now more than ever you will need to flip that script. Right now you are automatically running belief system programs. You have used these beliefs all your life as your basic operating system. Know this: these programs may prove faulty in times of trauma. They may very likely no longer be valid. The very first flip of your script will be to stop asking "Why?" and start asking "How?" How can I make this the best thing to happen to me? How can I find the joy in this?

Somewhere in this, the walls of your life fall down around you. You stand alone, looking out at what was and now the crushing reality of what is. The past is gone; the future is hazy. Uncertainty rules the day.

The question is, what has awakened in you because of this crisis? Does hope beat in your chest when you think of your future? Do you feel the sweet promise of tomorrow pulsing in you? Does everything you've taken for granted come sharply to clarity? Do you see your value? Do you feel the relevancy of your life? You now have the opportunity to become reacquainted with what makes you feel, as the numb shroud of your harried life falls away. Can you feel your passion? Can you begin to trace its origin?

You want to go back to feeling deeply, feeling good, and feeling better. It helps to quickly go to the root of your life challenges. It is better to treat yourself first as a whole person: the cause before the effect.

The Cold Hard Facts

Now is the time
To seize and begin again
Washed anew
Old vanities cut away
Literally

My sister Nikki, my mom and I were talking over my mother's dining room table. We were trying to wrap our heads around the drastic turn my life had taken. I was speaking about how unhappy I was with my current doctor's care plan. I said I would be seeking another doctor.

"Are you sure you're making the right decision, honey? He may not have the best bedside manner but I understand he is highly respected in his field," my mother said, concern in her voice.

I thought about how that same callous surgeon just prescribed me over 300 heavy-duty pain pills. It shocked and overwhelmed me. I felt he was telling me 'this really sucks. If I were you I would just get numb and stay there.'

"Mom, I told you that I do not like this doctor. Tell her, Nikki, how horrible he was when we went for the last consultation."

My sister spoke up, "She's right, Mom, and he's completely devoid of any compassion. He's exasperating and combative every time we ask a simple question. He has a major God-complex and doesn't think that we should dare ask him any questions at all. The woman has to undergo another major surgery and sacrifice her facial nerve. These fools were completely unprepared for what they found. I think she might have some questions!"

Mom nodded her head saying, "Okay, okay, but I hope you know what you're doing. I'd rather have a doctor who is capable instead of just nice."

I spent the next three weeks seeking several second opinions. I asked in every which way if there was any chance that I might smile again. I begged for a glimmer of hope. Was there any alternative other than disfigurement? I questioned what my chances of survival were. I discovered how nasty this cancer really was and ultimately found a different surgeon, the right one for me.

Dr. Costantino, my new doctor and surgeon, was connected to me by just a few degrees of separation. My brother Brad has a way of always knowing the right someone for any given emergency. It turned out his friend's older brother was a doctor who assisted in the same trauma ward during 9/11 with Dr. Costantino. Now Dr. Costantino would be helping me, thank goodness for that. He and his very special team, Clarita, Claudia, and Jules, speak the most excellent language of hope.

None of the news I sought with so much hope turned out to be good. Dr. Costantino, with his honest face and soft eyes, was straight up with me: "Michele, I wish I could tell you something different, but the reality is that Adenoid Cystic Carcinoma of the Parotid Gland is a rare and aggressive kind of cancer. If caught early it is dealt with by a simple course of radiation. This cancer is a killer if it isn't caught early."

"What do you mean aggressive? I thought it was a slow growing cancer?" I murmured.

Dr. Costantino replied, his eyes speaking volumes of heavy experience, "It is aggressive in that statistically it has a high likelihood of returning within the first 10 years. It can lie quietly for years and come back. It can return in the same area and then after radiation the only alternative is surgery. It can also come back in the lungs or the brain, all tough areas in the arena of fighting cancer."

I was told again that it could lie in wait for any number of years and return. If I survived I would be looking at 10+ years of tracking signs of its dreaded return.

Dr Constantino said, looking dead serious, "As you know your facial nerve needs to be removed, and perhaps other things as well. I do not know how far the cancer has traveled. I would like to be able to have a neurosurgeon on hand in case we encounter anything needing his expertise. Would that be okay with you?"

I nodded my head; it felt as heavy as lead. I listened to Dr. Costantino's kind voice, "Michele you understand that your face will be paralyzed. In many cases I can provide a sling to the remaining nerve endings and there is a greatly increased chance of facial movement recovery. I am sad to say that I do not believe this will be one of those cases. From the films I have seen and what I can make out from the surgical notes, the cancer is greatly involved in your facial nerve. I believe everything will need to go if we want to save your life."

I listened, cloaking myself in numbness; I sat very still and stared into Dr. Costantino's face. He gazed at me compassionately, "Honey, you are in good hands; we are going to take care of you. I want you to understand the realities. You will most likely drool when you eat. Your speech will be affected. Your smile and appearance will be greatly affected. Your eye will not be able to close on its own. We will be surgically implanting a gold weight into your upper eyelid. It will facilitate the eye closing enough for sleep and its very basic lubrication."

I looked through him seeing flashes of my life, and feeling freedom being smothered. I felt the bliss of believing I would live forever, slipping away. I was facing what people face in their 70s and 80s. I was going to walk around looking like a stroke victim forever. The rest of my life would be affected.

Dr. Costantino said in a nurturing voice, "Honey, I know how hard it is to never look the same again. It has been said that your smile is your passport to the world. It allows you entry like no other thing. It soothes people and helps others to smile back. I know what a harsh reality this is."

I looked down, feeling the prickle of tears burning. I thought, *so the choice is death or deformity, and even then I am guaranteed nothing*. I began to feel the hopelessness and despair seeping into my very core, searing me to the bone. I wanted to scream and rant and rave and give up, all at the same time.

Then I heard Dr. Costantino say, "I'm going to do my best to make sure you're around for your daughter's wedding." He paused, looking deeply into my eyes.

He had said exactly the right thing. My daughter had been born six months prior and thank God for her. We named her Sage and that is just what she is. She was a gift. My father had passed away the year before after a serious battle with cancer. I found out I was pregnant four months after he passed and out popped a replica of him. What are the chances that two black people would have a baby with blue eyes and sandy blond hair just like my dad? I look into Sage's eyes and I know my dad is here. Through my daughter, he helps me to stay strong, to know that I am equipped for this and any circumstance of life. I am not my smile; it is not my beauty. I am an amazing woman who is marked and yet ready to rise above the mark.

"You are reacting quite stoically to a life altering reality and I want to make sure that you are fully clear on the serious nature of it and the impact this is going to have," continued Dr. Costantino in a calm, even tone.

It was then, staring into his kind eyes, that I got hit with what felt like a tidal wave. My emotions swept through me. My shoulders began to shake. I felt flashes of blind hope, fear and visions of life going on without me. I sobbed and began to weep.

"I want to move forward as quickly as we can and as you will allow, Michele," Dr. Costantino said. "The cancer site has been cut into during the first surgery. Once cancer is disturbed it can begin to grow in any number of directions."

I felt a flash of anger at the incompetence of my last set of doctors. This very statement was completely contrary to the course that the last surgeon had prescribed. I remembered how the last surgeon said, "Ms. Howe, this cancer has been growing in you for years. Your other doctor and I can't coordinate our schedules until Memorial Day at the earliest. It is slow growing so waiting another couple of months would not make a difference."

I was fairly seething. This was just one more indication of how utterly callous he had been. It did not matter to him one iota. He could make me wait as if I had all the time in the world when in reality my life was actually hanging in the balance. He knew I was a woman facing disfigurement but hey, no rush; let's just let that life sentence hang out there for a couple of agonizing months.

Dr. Costantino roused me from my dark thoughts asking, "Will the day after tomorrow work for the surgery?" I looked at him in disbelief. "Or we could do it in just over a week?"

I nodded, "How about next week?" That should be long enough to digest and say good-bye to my beautiful smile, my passport to normalcy.

During that week, my brother Brad came over and took pictures. He is an avid photographer. He always has the newest equipment. He wanted to capture my smile while I still had it. My brother, always practical, as well as a talented photographer, said, "We better take some last pictures of you as you are now." He took some lovely photos of me smiling with my daughter, Sage, just a wee babe of six months. She made the taking of those pictures easier to bear. The context of this photo shoot was so surreal that no one really wanted to take it on. We just went through the motions, but it was all out of whack.

I could see Dwayne letting himself be drawn into the familiar ritual. He began smiling the programmed camera smile. I knew Dwayne certainly was not one to let his guard down or to show vulnerability. My brother clicked away, asking for Sage's attention. Dwayne kept the smile pinned to his face, but as the shots progressed tears filled his eyes until he just could not smile anymore.

Sages: One Old, One New

Sometimes it takes looking
Into a very young face
To show you life
Through wise old eyes

Dr. Costantino had said exactly the right thing to help me find meaning in this. He had shone a light for me. He said we were fighting to see me at my daughter's wedding. Sage, my sweet angel, would make my way to the future. If all else in the future looked dim, the image of Sage growing into herself shone brightly.

She was just a tiny little bundle when all this drama was going on around her. She was sweetly oblivious. Thank goodness for her levity. Sage too, came to us in an emergency scene at a hospital.

When it was confirmed I was pregnant, Dr. B., my OBGYN, said to Dwayne and I, "The image of your fetus from the sonogram does not look good. The fetus does not seem to be positioned correctly to sustain pregnancy." Dwayne and I stared blankly back at him. If I was ever unsure about having a baby, in that moment I knew I wanted to keep this child. I looked into Dwayne's eyes. I saw the same love for our child. I had a hard pregnancy. When I was past due by a week, I went to see the OBGYN, Dr. B. He said, "I am concerned, the baby seems very large. I want you to come into the hospital tonight and get induced."

Dwayne and I looked at each other. I wanted to have natural childbirth. "Can we think about it?" I asked.

"Of course, but you know my recommendation."

Dwayne pierced me with a look, I nodded silently. Dwayne said, "We will do what is best for our child. What time do you want us at the hospital?"

We arrived at the hospital three hours later. Doctor B. came and inserted a ribbon into my cervix to help soften the uterus. Then he hooked up monitors all over my swollen belly. We could see the lights of the baby's heart beating and breathing. All night I watched as the monitors reading my baby's pulse swung erratically from low to normal. I asked the night nurse, "Why does the baby's pulse read so low?" She looked at the monitor and then adjusted the monitor pads stuck to my belly. The pulse picked up. "You must have moved the monitors away from clearly reading the pulse. You must be careful not to move." I nodded but inside I didn't exactly buy it. None of the monitors had moved from where they were placed.

The next morning Dr. B. came in on his rounds. He asked, "How are you reacting to the ribbon? Having any contractions?" He measured my cervix. I was not dilated. "Michele, we'll give you some more time but if your cervix does not dilate in a couple of hours, I recommend a Caesarean."

Dwayne was also concerned with the baby's pulse reading throughout the night. Just as Dr. B. was leaving, Dwayne asked, "What would happen if the baby's pulse reading was low?"

Dr. B. said, "I would look at this machine and see that…" his voice trailed off. Then he continued, his voice raising in alarm, "Your baby is not breathing."

I began to cry. I said, "I told the night nurse, but she said I must have moved." Dr. B. and a senior nurse stood on either side of my belly as I lay looking up at their faces. They each had a monitor skimming my belly, looking for a breath reading. When they heard nothing, they looked at each other. Then everything went into fast forward.

The doctor screamed, "STAT! STAT!" and ran from the room, a nurse following him with scrubs. In the next moment, blue suited hospital staff came out of the woodwork. I was laid on a stretcher and run through the hall into the OR. Sage was born about a minute later. Dwayne did not even have time to get into the operating room. He was still putting on his scrubs when a harried nurse strode out of the OR with a squalling baby. "Here's your daughter. The mother is fine." Dwayne's eyes were full of tears as he first held and gazed at his perfect baby girl.

We named her Sage. That is just what she is. She looks out at the world with these shockingly blue/green gentle eyes that seem to know all the wisdom of the ages. She is such a love bug. Not one person can meet Sage without wanting to take her home. She just has this kind of magic. She casts a spell of sweetness that can soothe the most embittered heart. One only has to be with her for a brief time before her infectious smile brings joy. She is a gift, a living reminder of my dad, in looks, eyes and coloring. My dad was called Sandy for his sandy brown hair and blue eyes. Now here is Sage, sandy as a summer day at the beach.

My father was a man who lived the American Dream. His name was Dr. Alfred Sidney Howe. He was a first generation American. His parents were from the Caribbean. He grew up in Brooklyn, NY, during a time in the 1940's when Trinidadians would stand together financially and buy their homes. At that time, it was said around his neighborhood, "Don't sell to a Trini, or soon they will own the whole block." His sister was one of the founders of the Bedford Stuyvesant West Indian Day Parade. That parade today draws over a million people.

Dad decided he wanted to be a doctor in a time when there were few black doctors. He went to a medical university in the US. He had very poor eyesight and wore thick eyeglasses. He could not see through a microscope. For this reason, he was not allowed to continue his medical studies in the U.S. My father was not one to be stopped. He found an accredited medical university in Switzerland. The school's degrees were accepted throughout the U.S. With the aide of contact lenses, he was able to continue his medical studies there.

He took all of his medical classes and exams in French. He did not even speak French when he arrived. My dad was the first to show me the example of the power of focused energy. When he set his mind to something there was no question that he would accomplish it. He met my mother in Lausanne, Switzerland. Ironically, they were two West Indians who ended up meeting halfway around the world. They had a whirlwind romance in Europe and were married.

After finishing his residency, he obtained a job as an attending physician in a hospital close to their new home on the South Shore of Long Island. When he arrived for his first day of work, the security guard stopped him saying, "All deliveries go in the side entrance." My dad shook his head and smiled, "I am no delivery man. I am an attending doctor here in this hospital." The man sputtered, "Excuse me sir," as he moved aside to let my dad pass.

My father taught us about taking ownership of our actions. His life story was one of consistent self-responsibility. His actions were deliberate and thought out. He held his children to the same high expectations he had held himself. We knew his success formula was proven so it was always torture when he was disappointed in me. He would take me into his study. He would clasp his hands under his chin and stare down at me with his piercing blue eyes. When he looked at me like that I just wanted to be better, to be more, and to make him proud.

Dwayne always tells the story of his first time coming to my house to attend a party. He had driven all the way from Boston to attend this party in my father's honor. When he rang the bell, my father made sure to answer. He stood in the doorway with his arms crossed. He pushed his glasses down. He stared Dwayne up and down with his intimidating gaze. Dwayne later told me, "Your dad's eyes told a million stories. I knew not to mess with his daughter. I can't wait till some poor fool comes knocking for Sage. You know how I'm going to act."

My Mom and Dad gave each of their children a steel rod of independence that runs straight down our backs. They made sure we were well educated; we each earned post-graduate degrees. They ensured we enjoyed and experienced the beauty of the land of our forefathers. We went to the Caribbean every year to swim in the sea. We became strong swimmers so we could ride the waves with our father.

Dad was a great body surfer, able to ride waves gracefully into the beach, even in rough seas. My dad made me so proud that I wanted so much to keep my connection to such a powerful force. His strength never seemed to fade even through his long battle with cancer. He just adjusted. He was a trooper. He was always there to listen. Each one of his children would come to seek his advice. He was truly wise in the ways of the world. He was the counsel for his whole extended family. Distant cousins and family members would travel and call seeking advice.

Seeing my father looking back at me in my daughter's eyes, I knew innately everything would work out. Somehow…someway…I would ride this wave just like my Dad taught me, gracefully to the shore.

Wild Child

Youth
The highs so uncontrollable
The lows so immeasurable
Soaring to the sky, reaching for the heavens
Plummeting to the dark depths of the sea
Striding up hill
Tumbling down
Wondering: always questioning
Tears filling eyes for unknown reasons
No one understanding.
You don't even understand yourself
There seems to be no home for you
So you take on the wait
But what are you waiting for?

The times when I could not sleep yet the world slept all around me, I would reminisce over some of my previous close calls in life. These were situations that I could point to and remember I had been lucky before. They reminded me I could be lucky again.

One time occurred when I was living and going to school in Madrid. Life was completely devil-may-care. I hung with a motley crew of wealthy American college students. While some were soaking in the culture, the crew and I were steeping ourselves in partying. "Dick and Coke" was our drink of choice. "Dick" was what the Castilian bartenders called Jack Daniels. Going to school in Madrid gave us the opportunity to travel around Spain a great deal. In addition, we would take weekend touring trips. I looked out on a scene of all my partying friends spread out on the banks of a river. Don't ask me which river or city in Spain. We were all laying on the grass, with bottles of wine, bread, fruit and cheese in between. We laughed deeply and boisterously, sharing good cheer. I had thought to myself; *Cool, this is like a scene from a movie.*

Over spring break of my second semester, my friend Tina flew in to Madrid from New York. Tina was always ready to go the distance for a party experience. She had come to travel with me to Lagos, Portugal. Lagos is a beautiful city by the beach, rich in history and tradition. The sea vistas were something to write home about. Tina and I lived the life. Every night we went out to dinner. Tina would toast, "to the good life," and we would toss it down. The alcohol flowed freely. We were generally up for whatever fun we could get our hands on.

We were short on cash as we totally overdid it every night. No restraint was placed on reward or gratification. Every day we would hit the beach and lounge around, eating lunch at a seaside restaurant. Drinking a little, smoking a little, but definitely focusing on recovering from the last night's overindulgence. Though we were determined not to, in desperation, we were just about to have to call our parents to send cash. Our strict new budget lasted all of half of one day.

One night after a hearty round of drinking and dancing, Tina and I were walking down the hilly streets of Lagos. The streets are old, narrow, and lined with cobblestones. This one wound downwards in a meandering fashion. We had a general idea of where our rented rooms were. It was in the early morning hours. The streets were dark and deserted. We could only hear the sound of our own footsteps.

We were laughing and talking, discussing the night's festivities. Tina was reminding me of the crazy dance move we had seen a local doing at the bar. Tina began to imitate the moves saying, "Come on baby, let's dance." I broke out in laughter, doubling over with the sheer force. As the laughter shook my body, I began to feel unsettled. My tummy was not feeling so good.

"Hey Tina, how close do you think we are? Me no feely too good," I said.

Tina turned to me. She saw I was not in good shape. "Okay, Miche, just hold steady. We'll have you home in a jiff."

Tina held me around the waist and hurried our steps. It seemed absurdly quiet all of a sudden. We both grew uncomfortable when the sound of footsteps came from behind us.

A man in his early thirties appeared at our side. He said with a heavy accent, "Is everything alright?" Tina laughed and said, "No worries, we got the situation handled."

"No really," the man persisted, "I am with the Red Cross. I can help you." He got into step beside us, carrying a biker's helmet. Tina and I glanced at each other acknowledging silently that we did not like this guy.

Tina crowded me closer to her side, "Really, sir, we do not need any help. We're doing just fine."

"One can always use some help," the man assured us. He stepped closer to me. Tina tried to side-step and I stumbled. The man came forward and took my arm. "I said I help!" his voice had gone up an octave. Tina let him take my arm, at a loss as to what to do. I moved closer to Tina, and the stranger pulled me away a little. "Hey, lady, do not worry. I mean no harm. Let me help," he said in halting English.

I looked at Tina and shrugged a little. All this being pulled back and forth was making me feel sicker. The man now appeared to be gently propelling me down the street. We all fell silent as we plodded forward. This felt a little less uncomfortable to me. I thought, *Okay, maybe this guy is not a creep after all.*

Just then, as if he felt our defenses go down, he pounced. His hand started to stroke me, moving in a sly fashion around my waist. He pulled me to him. His hands seemed to be all over my body at once, especially groping my breasts. I tried to pull away.

Tina, realizing what was happening, hurled herself at him screaming, "Get your hands off my friend, you pervert!" She lunged at him. I began to scream. I have one set of lungs when I put them to work. Boy, oh boy, that night I made sure as hell I could be heard LOUD and clear.

Tina got in one good shove at the lust-crazed predator before she stumbled and fell to the ground. The man was back on me in an instant. Tina gave an adrenalin-filled growl as she prepared to lunge at him again. She began to rise and run towards him, but he spun around, hitting Tina in the face with his helmet.

The sound was bone cracking. Tina flew backwards and lay still on the ground. I could hear her groaning, but she seemed unable to get up again. I let out another howling scream. This time it was answered by an approaching car. Our assailant's eyes filled with fear. He turned and fled the scene, disappearing as fast as he had appeared.

I, now sober as a rock, knelt to help Tina up. As I bent down, I saw Tina's eye was swelling shut; a trickle of blood fell from the corner. From what I could see, Tina's eye was blood red. There was terrible swelling on her cheekbone. I sighed, "Thanks a lot for fighting for me, Tina. Sorry he was such a malicious bastard."

Tina replied in a shaken voice, "What a dick to hit a woman. He makes me sick."

The car we had heard approaching pulled up along side us. It was a taxi driver. "What happened ladies?" he asked.

I said, "Some sick man just tried to attack us."

The taxi driver shook his head at us. "You two should know better. There is a rapist running around these streets. You should consider yourself lucky that all you got was a black eye."

I shook my head at the stupidity of youth. Tina and I always thought we were ten feet tall and invincible. I tried to remember this youthful, exuberant confidence when I discovered my dire survival statistics.

Goodbye Smile

I need to forge a way forward
With hope and love
I am afraid
But I choose not to live in fear
This is my time for I am Present
For
Life in every breath
My spirit is my own
I will practice in the present
Find joy in the now
It is all that is real

I spent the next ten days before the second operation, analyzing my life. I reflected on all that I had been to that point: the rebel in high school, one of the few minority students. I did, said and wore what I wanted. I remember being so carefree and so confident. I had had a drink in my hand on weekends since I was 16, always organizing my group of friends to go to parties and bars.

In college, I was a tulip-bell bottom-jumpsuit wearing, beaded-braid, hippie girl-woman who rocked my way through four years as a social butterfly. College was all about self-discovery and partying. I was always in motion. I surrounded myself with people. A butterfly was exactly how I saw myself in college. I couldn't walk ten feet without greeting every other person. I always presented a big smile, glowing with enthusiasm, a pure people-pleaser.

I got so good at people-pleasing that I lost touch with exactly what I needed. Then, I lost track of what I should be pleased about. I had really honed my partying skills when I spent my junior year abroad in Madrid. I had traveled all over Europe with a bunch of bad-ass, privileged Americans.

After graduating college and spending a year traveling across America, I headed down to DC. Though saying goodbye to Dwayne was harsh, I knew I was not long for Boston. He would have to man up and follow me. I, of course hoped to make the urge to join me irresistible. I always wanted to live with my sister Nikki so I moved into Nikki's apartment. I also stepped neatly into Nikki's old legal assistant job at a downtown DC tax law firm. The naming partner was a riotous man who was always good for a laugh. He was a character to say the least.

During that time, my big sister Sydney had a conversation with me over the kitchen table at 180 Bayview, where many transformative conversations had been held before. This conversation changed the course of my life. Sydney simply suggested that I had always been one to take risks. It seemed to her that since I was a natural at math, I would do well in an MBA program. I leapt at the idea. I felt I needed some direction in life. Sydney was always good at helping me steer straight. She even made me stay weekends at her apartment during my first year at BU so I did not flunk out.

I studied for and took the GMAT. I was overjoyed to be accepted into Howard University's MBA program. I took to finance like a charm. I rose to the top of my class. My first year, I received an internship at the Export Import Bank of the United States. I also won a scholarship to the Center for Professional Development. The Center was headed by the fantastically enthusiastic Harold Gray. I became class president. I was awarded a Phi Beta Kappa. In my final year I enthusiastically drummed up support for an MBA Exclusive event in which many new corporations came to recruit MBA graduates.

I decided to go into banking, investment banking to be precise. I would go deep within corporate America and understand its inner workings. I also knew that over time I would be compensated at the highest rate possible. Dwayne had moved down to DC and we were living together. He was working at a downtown club as the head chef. One night after a brutal associate position rejection from a top investment bank in New York City, he asked me to marry him. I was drinking vodka that night and there was no stopping me as I danced and sang reggae in our living room. As I belted out my anger and frustration at the world, Dwayne took a deep breath. He knew it was time to ask this crazy vivacious woman to be his wife.

I landed a job at an investment banking firm. I began working 120 hours a week. I soon became a serious drinker. I could hang with the best of them. Drinking became my favorite past time. If there was a sunny day, the city parks would not be the first thing on my mind, but rather which open-air bar I would go to. Drinking, smoking, socializing and shopping were my only hobbies. I was constantly on the phone talking to friends, laughing and planning some get-together. My social group had always been my highest priority, ever since I was old enough to have friends.

I was always making new friends. I constantly reached out to new people. Why not, my life was damn near perfect. I had no fear of rejection. I called and organized people constantly. I made sure I did not lose a friend, even if I had to take some of their shit. All my friends were pleasing to look at too. What a coincidence.

I surrounded myself with others who also shared my love of drink. We deserved it, didn't we? We were investment bankers after all. We all worked hard. Besides that, we could afford it.

Given my success at people-pleasing, it was no wonder I was a high earner. Yet, I was giving myself away. I made it to the Ivy League of professions where I rose from grunt analyst to Vice President in five short hard-drinking years.

For seven years I rewarded myself with jewelry, clothes, vacations, food, smoke, a country house; and, yes, yes, the drink. Along the way, I got married and had a little girl. Still I dreamed of independence.

Of course, all of that working hard and playing hard had a price. I never dreamt how high a price. Every time I made up my mind to take another route, some new lure would come my way shackling me tighter in the "golden handcuffs" of my professional life. I remember crying in the shower and in the stairwells at work.

I had always been hard on myself. I was constantly criticizing myself in my head. I told my body I would take care of it soon. This diet or that pill would solve it. I always had so much to do. There was always some other goal to reach that was more important than my health. Not to mention that I loved to party. The gremlin inside would remind me every time I passed a mirror that I was a lazy slouch, and there was no hope for me. I would leave my soul at home most days just to make it through work.

At work I had no confidence because I felt I was hiding who I really was. I was never comfortable at work. I thought for sure my colleagues would not respect me if I showed them my true self. I clothed myself in what I thought was their perception of me. I began to feel empty. The only thing that made me feel excited about life was excess. I had become a narcissistic hedonist.

Momentary Lapse

There are moments when
All reason is lost
A mind howling at the moon
Rabid with a wildness
Of heart

The night before the operation I could not sleep at all. I couldn't imagine my life without a smile. It was a long night, one of the longest nights of my life. I knew everything would change, indisputably, the next day. There was no going back.

The next year would be harder than anything I had ever faced. Thoughts raced around my head unbidden. I knew I had to be strong, but stronger than all this heavy-duty hard-core reality? How long would this abyss of darkness go on? Where would we land? Is this what it feels like to be drowning?

I shook my head. *No,* I said to myself mentally, *I am not going down that road.* I filled my mind with old stories. They reminded me of the stuff I was made of. I remembered my tattoo. It's a griffin. It's a fuzzy blue creature on my ankle. It looks like an old seaman's tattoo. The tattoo drill and needles used to make it were about that archaic.

I had gone to visit my sister Nikki at George Washington University in Washington, DC during her sophomore year. I was a freshman myself at Boston University. I was now 18, so almost all decisions were mine. How sweet that was. During the week I visited with my sister I stayed with a friend of mine.

My friend Marjohn lived in a beautiful part of Maryland, just outside of DC. I was enjoying myself but I was restless and felt stir crazy outside of the city. I just wanted action 24/7. Wherever the party was, I would be there.

It was a hot spring day. DC has amazing weather just before the summer locks in the heat and humidity. Marjohn and I were supposed to visit the museums and monuments. Her parents thought it would be a wasted trip to the Nation's capital, so steeped in history, if I did not at least see some of it. We were late in leaving and did not really want to go at all if anyone cared to ask our opinion. I was on the bed moaning, "We should have freedom of choice. We are adults now. It's not fair to waste such a great day in a stuffy old museum."

Marjohn smiled at me conspiratorially. "You know, no one has to know what we do today. Let's escape and do something we've only dreamt about." Marjohn was always one to push the envelope. I, too, really believed what I preached. Marjohn was always about going for the gusto. She was no holds barred. Her philosophy was just do it.

Marjohn asked me, "So Miche, this is your spring break after all. What is your most wicked, risqué desire?"

I did not have to think long before I said, "The hell with museums, I want to get a tattoo." In a flash, Marjohn was there with the yellow pages. She looked up tattoo parlors. She called the closest one. "Hi, we would like to get a tattoo today?" I waited with bated breath, and then I heard Marjohn say, "Okay then, we'll see you in an hour." Marjohn turned to me and we squealed with delight.

We drove to the tattoo parlor—both a little quiet, tasting our power as adults. I was about to mark myself for life, without asking anyone's opinion or permission. We arrived at our destination. We found ourselves staring at a dingy, one-bedroom house (although a shack might have been a better description!). We looked at each other, both having second thoughts. By the looks of things this tattoo artist had obviously not done well for himself.

Just as we were about to speak, a fat, middle-aged man with stringy hair came out of the house. "Are you my two o'clock appointment? You know I do not accept cancellations, so you will have to pay me for my time, anyway. Come in and take a look at the designs," he said. His voice crackled from many a smoke-filled night shouting at the bartender for another round. As we got closer, I could see that his white T-shirt was stained with sweat rings. I felt disgusted.

The tattoo man had some jailhouse-looking, do-it-yourself variety tattoos on his forearms. On his upper arms he had more professional navy-type tattoos. They all appeared to have been done before the tattoo craze had swept the country. There were new artists emerging, but I did not know what qualities to look for in a tattoo artist. The importance of a sanitary environment had not occurred to us.

He grunted, "Do you have a design in mind?"

I looked around nervously, "Not really. I thought I would pick one from your stock."

The man looked miffed. He probably had a 5th calling his name from the back room. He said, "Well, hurry up, I don't have all day."

I was fully committed to the idea by now and nothing was going to dissuade me from making this tattoo a reality. I began skimming the walls with my eyes, taking in all the usual early tattoo designs: a red rose with thorns, a cross, swords, dragons, and cartoons.

I could feel the time ticking away. Nothing was appealing to me. I cleared my throat. I asked the burly, booze-smelling, ex-sailor posing as my would-be tattoo artist, "Do you have any other art?"

The man was beginning to look really pissed now. "Yeah, but hurry it up or just pay me now and go. I got things to do."

"Okay, okay. Let me see the books," I said, getting a little upset by the disgruntled man's rude behavior. By now I was committed to the venture. I was not about to let anything stand in my way; not the rude tattoo artist or the sinking feeling in my stomach that warned me to wait. After all, I might be able to find a better artist. Or, I could even think a bit about what kind of tattoo I wanted to mark my body for the rest of my life.

Marjohn was no help. She just stood back looking entertained. She said, "Miche, I can see he will not have time for me to get one today, so I will just let you get yours." I turned harried eyes to see Marjohn looking relieved not to be on the receiving end of this dirty man's needle. I just nodded and kept searching.

The pickings were slim. The photo albums of designs housed nothing new, nothing that inspired me. The man came out and fairly screamed, "If you do not decide on a design in the next minute or so, I want to be paid and you can be on your way."

"Okay, okay," I sighed. I wondered if I could ever find anything in this pile of mediocrity.

Just then a picture of a griffin caught my eye. I liked the ruggedness of this mythical creature. *Half lion half eagle,* I thought, *ruler of both land and sky.* I liked it. It would be something to protect me and remind me of how strong I was. I was the ruler of my life. This would represent that I could always take care of myself, no matter what. I was satisfied that I could embrace this design and concept for the rest of my life.

"I found one," I motioned to Marjohn, showing her my griffin and explaining what it would mean to me. Marjohn shrugged her shoulders and nodded, "I like it, Miche. Make the call." I called to the tattoo man.

"Let me see it," he said as he glanced at the griffin. "Okay, I can do this. Where do you want this?" I was caught again, unprepared to answer right away. I knew I wanted it somewhere visible to others. It also had to be easily visible from my vantage point. On a whim I chose my left lower calf right above my ankle. "Here," I pointed.

The man raised and eyebrow and smirked at me, "You know that is going to hurt like a bitch, don't you?" I wouldn't let him see me flinch.

"Yeah, well, this is where I want it. Can you handle it?" I challenged.

"Give me the design", he said, "I will have to photo copy it. What size did you want?" I circled my pointer finger and thumb indicating a 50-cent-piece-sized circle. He laughed and said, "My photo copier can only shrink it down to about two inches by three inches. After that, lines get blurred and I can't see the trace lines."

"You have to trace it onto my leg; you can't do it free-style?" I taunted.

"Hey, lady, I tattoo. I'm not Picasso," he smirked.

"Alright, alright," I said, my frustration with this jackass beginning to wear my patience down. He photocopied it down to 2" x 3". It took him six reductions. By the time it was that small, the lines were thick and blurry.

I had released all worries by this time. What would be would be. I gave myself over to the situation. I watched as he wet the photocopy and placed it above my left ankle. I heard the buzzing of the needle. I noticed that he did not clean off the needle before pushing it into my skin. I felt the raking sensation as the needle moved at lightning speed in and out of the flesh of my ankle. I felt the burning pain, the sensation of fire searing the needle's course. A line of blood bubbled up from underneath my skin. When he wiped the blood away, I sighed with pleasure as my griffin began to take its shape.

One hour later, I had a fuzzy griffin tattooed into my skin. The blood had not fully dried, but I could already see the black ink turning a navy blue. The lines were beginning to bleed ink into the surrounding skin. I knew my griffin would not be perfect. I did not care. It was mine. I had made my first resolute decision as an adult. I flinched internally when I thought about how much my parents would not like this. "Well it's better than dropping out of college," I muttered defiantly to myself. I was prepared to defend this decision, no matter how irresponsible or rash it might have been.

Cut It Out

I awake afraid
Go to sleep hesitant
I grant myself time
Let myself grieve
It is time for truth
Risk at all cost
Too young to face mortality

The day of my second surgery had arrived. We were waiting in the pre-surgery room. It was early and I had not slept much; my mind was racing. Dwayne was holding my hand, absent-mindedly thumbing through a magazine. He would be in the neurosurgery waiting room. This time, at least, he knew he was in for a long wait. Some of my family would arrive later that day. This second operation could take upwards of nine hours. *I cannot believe this is happening to me! What the hell am I going to do? This is some seriously scary shit*, I thought pensively.

I knew the doctor warned me that my eye would not blink after the surgery. He said I should prepare myself to have a gold weight sewn into my eyelid to help me close my eye. It was unbelievably scary to contemplate not being able to close my eyes. Sometimes one must be able to shut everything out.

As the operation loomed closer, I had major trepidation. I even considered not going in and just running away and smiling to death. Young, beautiful, and dead; no way, I held strong. As I was wheeled into the operating room, I broke down and started to cry. I truly knew fear. It was cold in the operating room. The stark metal lights above my head blinded me. The anesthesia tasted weird. It made my body so heavy that there was nothing to do but go into the void. I blacked-out knowing I would never be the same again.

When I awoke my body was shaking. I shook uncontrollably. I could not make it stop shaking. It was very scary, but the staff knew it was the anesthesia. They stabilized my body with a shot of something. I was too out of it on morphine to even care what it was.

I went in and out of consciousness. Then my brother and Dwayne appeared. They were smiling down conspiratorially at me like little schoolboys. Brad smirked, "We snuck past the nurses. We just wanted to see you so badly." In my stoned mind I giggled with them, but in reality I was just lying there motionless, staring out, numb. A nurse promptly appeared winking, "Okay busters, you got what you came for. So come back, like good boys, during visiting hours."

I had decided to take a single luxury room because hey, I was going through hell, why share it with some other person? I was going to have filet mignon, cable TV and video rentals, the whole nine yards. I had the money. I still had the investment banker mentality, so that was how I proceeded.

The second operation was a major one, removing all the branches of my facial nerve and more cancerous growth from my temple down into my shoulder muscle. The wound was now quite large and gaping. I had to spend the first night in Neuro ICU. Dwayne, who had been staying with me in my private suite, could not stay the night in ICU. I felt so alone. I was scared.

There was one nurse there who was very compassionate and cheerful. Thank goodness for her. She was amazing. Unfortunately, it felt like her assistant had some kind of vendetta against me. She did everything she could to inflict pain on me. I couldn't speak, I couldn't move. My whole head had been split open. Not only had they found cancer in the facial nerve, it went all the way up to my temporal bone, approaching my brain on the right side. They had cut me open from the top of my head all the way down my neck. They had sewn and stapled me back together.

The nurse's aide jarred the IV stem attached to my hand. She must have known how much pain I was in and how scared I was. She was careless and negligent. I was in a lot of pain and my speech was slurred. My face was so swollen it hurt to speak.

I managed to whimper, "Please, don't touch my IV." The aide just smiled viciously, grabbed my IV hand and gave it a good squeeze. My eyes crossed with pain. Then I fell into a morphine sleep. I began to feel like my life was a surreal experience.

The next morning I awoke in the ICU to find two fellows leaning over me. "We are ready to put that gold weight into your eyelid to help it close." I looked at them confused. Was I imagining it or was my eye closing?

Dwayne walked into the ICU just then. He saw that I looked concerned. "What's going on?" he asked.

"We are going to perform a minor surgery on your wife to insert the gold weight, which will help her eye close. It is very minor and we will not be using the OR, just a small patient's room we use for minor procedures."

Dwayne looked deeply into my eyes and we communicated silently. He said, "Blink, honey." I looked back at him and blinked my misting eyes. He smiled, "I thought I saw your eye blinking yesterday."

"Me too," I chimed in, glad he could read me so well and that I was not dreaming. My eye could still close! That was something, at least …

The fellow leaned forward. "Show me," he said. I closed my eye. He looked somewhat surprised. He said, "Close them again." I did. "Hold it closed." I did. He, being a doctor of Western medicine, said, "Don't get your hopes up. It will stop working; it's just a matter of time. You would be better off just letting us do it now. Having an unblinking eye is no fun."

Dwayne and I exchanged glances and silently agreed, "I'll take that chance. Thanks, anyway." The miracle was that my eye was closing. It was not blinking like the other side but it closed and it stayed closed enough for me to go to sleep. The doctors were amazed. Maybe I had some surprises up my sleeve yet. They had been so ready to slit open my eyelid and shove a little gold weight in there, I wondered, *how much harder would that little weight have made it for me to keep my eye open*? But thankfully, my eye was working.

I stayed in the hospital for six days after this second operation. I had a shunt pulled out of the artery in my pelvic area by a P.A., a physician's assistant. He was young and cocky. He just grabbed the shunt hose as if it were a garden hose and yanked. I said, "Hey, that really hurts!" He raised an eyebrow quizzically asking, "Really?" I nodded vigorously. He just shrugged and said, "It shouldn't." I swore to myself, *What a dick you are, you little prick.*

I spent the next days in the hospital healing from this radical surgery with a shunt coming out of my head oozing fluid. I have very "bad veins" as they call them in the medicalese. This means they are small, deep and hard to find. I had to take a lot of IV antibiotics. There were many people trying to find veins. One day, I had about five people poking around in me trying to find a vein. The aggressive P.A.s continuously shoved needles into me. One young woman said, "Well, if all else fails we can always find a vein in your hand. It is much more painful but it gets our job done." *Arrgh,* I thought, *this girl is just checking boxes off her to-do list.* This mechanical, callous attitude made me want to shoot them.

When having my stitches removed from my ear area, the young female P.A. had no finesse. She snipped inside my ear; it hurt like a bitch and I said, "You cut me." She just looked at me like "What?!" I pointed to the area she just cut and, lo-and-behold there was blood. Her eyes widened at the sight.

She turned guiltily to the attending fellow; her shoulders went up in a shrug. *Ooops, onto the next hapless Guinea pig*, I seethed inwardly.

The doctor took over removing the stitches. In that moment I realized I had to speak up and ask for what I needed. From here on out, I decided, no more inexperienced P.A.s would be working on me. I always wonder if that snip was the beginning of my insane infection. The fissure showed up in that exact area. More on that later.

I had been lying in the hospital bed for a couple of days. My face was stitched up. I had a shunt sticking out of the side of my face. Staples ran along half my head. It was very painful. I had gradually folded myself into such a position where I actually looked like I had a hunchback. I was all scrunched to one side. I was instinctively protecting my injured side, shielding it from further harm. A young doctor, one of the fellows on Dr. Costantino's team, had a great personality. I asked him half jokingly, "Hey Doc, will I ever get straightened out?" He leaned down as if to give me a consoling pat, but instead firmly took my head and shoulder, abruptly gave me a strong push in each direction. Voila, I was straight again. "Yes," he said with a mischievous grin. It felt so good to be straight I actually grinned back.

That young cocky surgeon with the dance song for a ringtone taught me something that I will never forget. Somewhere along the way, after the second operation, I wanted to know what my prognosis was. The previous doctors were so unprepared during the first surgery they couldn't stage me. They could not tell me where I was other than that the cancer had aggressively grown and was in the late stages. When I pressed this doctor to give me a sense of what my future looked like, and my prognosis, he said, "You are not a statistic. There is only a 100% chance or a 0% chance. You are one person, so it's all or nothing." That really helped me to get my mindset away from what the statistics say is the medical truth. I began to move in a new direction and rely on myself. I became the captain of my health care team. Go Team Michele!

Your Choice

Saving your life is all or nothing. You need to be in it to win it. Your chances are either 0% or 100%. It is your choice how you perceive the facts. When you got the bad news it's a good sign if your will surged forth crying out for life. You are here, living, real. You made it. You were born. Think about it "How many people have ever been born from the beginning of time?" You are one of them. Congratulations, you are worthy. Be confident in that which beats your heart. Know you have an inner self. You have a higher self that is omnipotent. The same power circulates your blood and fills your lungs. Be optimistic. Only lack of confidence will obstruct you. Whatever you desire you must have faith in it. If you don't believe in it, your subconscious will follow that feeling. Remember, you will find what you expect, be optimistic

If your body, mind and emotions are not in agreement, then your goal will not be authentic to you. You want to keep your body, mind and emotions as balanced as possible. You can be whatever you want. You just have to decide. In decision lies confidence. Be assured that you are able. Visualize yourself as you desire to be. Have beautiful dreams and visions. Really feel as if you achieved your desire and are living it now in the present. Feel the pleasure of having received it. Let these positive emotions flow.

Reminders Of The Past

Photographs
Holograms to the past
Yielding memories and feelings
So potent they are almost
Tangible

Photographs
A moment caught in a still frame
Turns back the hands of time
To a moment that once was
And now is only a feeling

When I got out of the hospital I went to stay at my mother's. I planned to stay there a month, but after a couple of weeks I had to leave. My mother lives in a house of mirrors. Mirror, mirrors, everywhere mirrors. I was surrounded by mirrors on all sides. It was like a house of horror. The person looking back at me in the mirror was a grotesque twisted version of me.

I was completely bloated on one side. My face was red like a cherry tomato and large acne was breaking out on my slack face. My face, at rest, just frowned at me; imagine a twisted harlequin. My eye stared back at me; a sad likeness of itself. When I spoke, laughed, or cried, the disparity between one side and the other was shocking to me. All my facial expressions were so grossly distorted.

I was taking pain medication and experiencing night terrors. Night terrors are the worst nightmares I could ever have imagined. I would rise up from sleep struggling to take a breath, my heart racing and adrenalin flooding my body. These nightmares made me wish I could return to the sweet bliss of my former life. I would awake from these nightmares to arrive in a waking nightmare. There was no escape. My deformed face was a reality. Death was a real possibility. Life could go on without me. Sage might never know her mother.

After a night or two of these horrific nightmares, I dreaded sleep and would fight it off. As all those around me faded and gave in to the urge to sleep, I would sit alone with my pain. I looked at the sleeping world and cried with rage. My whole life had changed so radically that I barely recognized what remained. I was on the other side of a destroyed bridge left with no one but myself. On one side of the bridge was every comforting thing I knew. I stood alone with no way back.

I stayed awake most nights. I had to sleep sitting up, because I had the shunt that needed to drain. There was no way for me to relax. Even Dwayne, who fought hard to stay awake with me, would sooner or later succumb to sleep. I was awake with only my fear and sadness to keep me company. When I shut my eyes all I saw were demons from hell. They just wanted to scare the living shit out of me. During those long sleepless nights I envisioned life going on without me, my daughter never knowing her mother. I felt alone, on a precipice, as the Earth I knew fell away beneath me.

Every time one of my immediate family members would leave to go home after visiting me during my stay at my mom's, I felt enraged and helpless. They got to leave the terror and horror behind and return to their normal lives. Normalcy had been taken from me. I was forever changed, visibly different and maybe not alive for much longer. *Wow, this sucks.*

I would watch movies only to cry when I realized there was no escape. My life would still be the same when the movie ended. Again and again, I came crashing back to the reality that my chance at perfection was gone. I felt abandoned by God. I also felt I had abandoned myself. I was in a foreign land. I had been removed from all things familiar. Nothing was easy anymore. There would be no more casual meetings, no easy acquaintances. The wake-up calls were just beginning for me.

In those long and lonely nights I came to the realization that I was the only one who could create a happy ending. I was the only one who had the power to heal myself. As I looked out at the world, I saw we all are twisted in some way. Some of us torture ourselves internally, like I used to. I had never been comfortable in my body. I was never totally happy being me. Cancer, and my subsequent disfigurement, pushed my imperfections to the forefront. It took away my ability to be egotistical. It ripped apart the narcissistic, material-driven, Myth of Perfection-woman I had become. I was thrust into a world of spirit, healing and intent. I was gifted with an abrupt ending so that I could begin again, from scratch. I shed layers of wasted self like the skin of an onion being peeled away.

Yucky Yuck #%&$!

I am the one here
All of this show is mine to experience
I shift and change
Bracing myself
I know now
It is I who will be here
Through it all
No one can do this job
I must for me
Only I can
Run this race
From start to finish

Four days after the second operation I discovered that I was leaking: green ooze was slowly coming out of my ear near the incision. I no longer had a normal ear. I had an ear that had been sewn back on. The blood flow to the area was less and my ear poked out from the side, like Dumbo. The green ooze had a foul odor to it. It was thick and yucky. My face was red and even more swollen than it had been. I called the doctor and asked hopefully, "Is this a normal part of the healing process?"

He said, "No, we need to see you. You need to go to the emergency room."

"How much of an emergency, right now or later this afternoon?" I had just gotten out of the hospital a few days ago. I was in no mood to return.

He said, "You need to be seen immediately. Someone will be on call waiting for your arrival."

Aiy! I thought, *that did not sound good.*

The doctor had said it should not be a long stay. I wanted to believe him. I operated on the notion that I would be in and out of the hospital. Well, that's not what happened. I went in, and I was in there for another two full weeks.

I could tell things were bad when I saw the alarm on the doctors' faces. One doctor said, "Michele, we're not happy to see this type of mucous excreting from within the inner operating site. We're going to fight this with the strongest IV antibiotics." I groaned, my eyes grew big with apprehension. The last thing I wanted was to be cooped up in the hospital for any amount of time. I knew what the doctors were going to say before they said it.

"To do that effectively, Michele," he continued, "we are sorry, but you will need to stay here in the hospital until we have this infection under control." Tears filled my eyes. I felt totally helpless and out of control. This sucked.

Again I was confined to a hospital room while the doctors tried to fight the infection with some strong IV antibiotics. I could actually taste them as they coursed through my body. I stayed again in a luxury suite. At least there I had relative peace and quiet—after all, everyone staying there was paying dearly for it. Down on the Neuro floor there were all kinds of disturbances;

like the man screaming bloody murder about seeing spiders. It turns out he just had brain surgery and this was an unexpected side effect.

I tried to find a comfortable space for me. Sydney, my eldest sister, came and performed Reiki on me. Reiki is the Japanese technique for stress reduction and relaxation that also promotes healing. While she was working over the energy centers I could swear I felt a sensation of a string pulling out of the infected area. I always felt more positive and lighter after a session. She, on the other hand, seemed like she took on some of my toxicity. I believe those sessions were draining on her because she gave so much of herself over to the Reiki healing for me.

I also tried meditation through chanting. I brought my ashram, a little temple, into the hospital room and gave offerings. I chanted with my sister Nicole, who chants regularly. She has found a real sense of strength and centered peace when she chants. She speaks the words so quickly it is like a blur of language. I was unable to keep pace with her, but I found a sense of good vibrations in attempting and in being close to someone who was connecting. Connecting to what? To the Source of all things, the Divine we all have in us. Just past the ego's chatter, you find the stillness within. Beyond the body's carnal desires, you reach the feeling of true abundance. Out of reach of the mind that just wants answers is the stirring of possibility. There we find our Source. It is a remembering of sorts.

I did not want to see anybody that hadn't been part of this ride from its tragic beginning. It was too much to re-tell. I was nowhere in sorting through any of it. It all felt too much to deal with. I wanted desperately to know why. *Why me? Why now? What the f***?* How was I going to live through this? What kind of Michele would survive? I found I needed time just to be alone and take it in. I wanted to let the whole experience just roll over me. It was better not to fight the tide of this huge tsunami attempting to overwhelm me.

Alone I could float better out there in the depths. I began to close down, to just stop thinking and planning. I hunkered down and got ready instinctively to get through this, come hell or high water. I needed to close a lot of chapters in my life that I had left hanging by tiny strings of regret. Whatever the reason, it felt right for me to lighten up on my internal responsibility to please the world.

With my small veins, I again had many people poking and prodding me, especially in the spot where they put the IV into my arm. My arm was not accepting it and was blowing up. I had a huge fight with Dwayne because I was not being a cooperative patient. "Michele, you know why they are doing this. To help you. Why do you have to make it so difficult for these people to help you?" He sounded exasperated. He looked so agitated. He was millimeters away from exploding.

I could feel the tears welling up in my eyes. My voice cracked with the force of my emotion. "They can't find my vein and now they are only fishing around with needles in my skin hoping to find one. They're making me bleed and they're just hurting me! There has to be a better way!" It was déjà vu of my last hospital stay. No one was trying to find another way. It was just the same shit, different P.A.

Dwayne just looked at me like I was crazy. "You're being a baby, Michele. Get your shit together. I can't take this anymore! I have to get out of here." He stormed out of the room.

I sobbed his name. I was terrified of being abandoned. The truth was that I was now disfigured. Dwayne was married to a woman whose face was half paralyzed. No matter how it was spun, I would never fit society's norms of beautiful ever again. His wife was now living with illness that few her age were prepared to cope with. Not only that, but the future, always so certain before, now was only a black abyss.

I cried out my agony. I sobbed out my helplessness. I wept out my fear. I knew again the statistics were not with my marriage either. I knew it would be very difficult for Dwayne now and in the future.

I also knew that if someone was hurting me, I was going to make a stink. I would not just sit by, a docile patient. Dwayne would have to deal with me standing up for myself in the medical establishment even if it was not the norm.

After a while, I fell into a deep cleansing sleep. When I awoke, I looked over to see Dwayne sleeping in his roll away bed. I sighed and decided not to worry about the strength of our relationship. He was right by my side through it all. His love never wavered. He stayed with me in my hospital suite every time except after the first operation when I shared a room with someone and the night in ICU. He was hanging tough with me.

I began to appreciate my blessings when and where they appeared. One such blessing was significant. Dwayne's parents, Hazel and Aundrea, were there for us. They came down for weeks at a time and helped with Sage. She was as tenderly cared for as if I were there. This allowed Dwayne to be at my side during these harrowing times and long hospital stays.

After five days in the hospital I got the most dreaded news. I knew I was not getting any better and the doctors were very concerned about the infection being located in such a sensitive area, so close to my brain and spine. I knew in my heart that surgery would be the only other alternative, but I was deep in denial by this time. There was no way I could fathom the need for another major head and neck surgery so soon after the two I had had in just a month.

I looked at the doctor wide-eyed, flecked with the last glimmers of hope. He shook his head imperceptibly. "Michele, the infection is not responding to antibiotics. I put you on a course of the strongest antibiotics available. It's just not able to reach that area due to low blood flow. An infection close to your head is never the best thing. We need to act quickly and remove whatever is infected."

I listened, still as a mouse. He listed all the scary things I was now prone to, like meningitis or the infection reaching my brain. Dr. Costantino caught my attention when he said, "There is a good side to this, Michele. Studies show it is a very good thing to have an infection around the site where cancer once was. It shows that your body is fighting and actively involved in that area."

A third operation?! I sunk into a pit of despair. I just could not cope with the idea of facing a third operation. It was all becoming too much for me.

The Story of You

One of the first things to understand is that there are the facts and then there is your story about the facts. The facts themselves are cold and clinical. It is the story you tell yourself about the facts that drives your emotions. The fact of being diagnosed with a disease is cold, unemotional. It is the story you tell about those facts that creates your experience.

Stand in your power. Learn how thoughts affect your feelings. First comes the thought, then the feeling. Know whatever modern convenience you can think of was first born as a thought in someone's mind.

Start the fascinating study of how you became you. You constructed your reality by listening to the narrator in your head. Life as you know it is a construction of memories and information you have collected. Memories consist of pictures, sounds and feelings.

If you are living defensively, you wake up every morning and go about life with beliefs that you happened to pick up along the way. You can now start to live purposefully and ask. Does this belief actually still work for me? If your beliefs do not support you, you can shift that to something that serves you.

I did the best I could under the circumstances. I brought in CDs that would give me inspiration. I did whatever distracted me. I read romance novels. I drew. I watched movies. My family visited me regularly during each hospital stay. Brad brought comic books and sketch pads, even bad tabloid magazines, was ready to assist in any way he could. My mom would just sit by and be there, offering herself. Sydney would lend herself to the situation; offering massages, Reiki, or help in the bath.

I did everything I could to just stay present in the moment. I tried not to let this relentless sense of despair overtake me. If I didn't, I was in for a long ride down a dark tunnel. I needed to move toward the light. Nikki came back and forth from Atlanta and chanted with me. Sometimes, when I couldn't keep going, she would carry on for me.

My cousin Anna flew in from Trinidad. It is very expensive to do that, but she came. We had lost contact. Our lives had grown apart. In our youth we were very close and spent a lot of time together. When she arrived, she brought herself as a resource. She stood by and was there for whatever was needed. In a time when I did not want to see anyone, her soft nature made her welcome. She held fast and stayed present. She is a truly beautiful gift of the best of humanity. She also left me a gift, a book, *How to Beat Cancer,* which had helped a friend of hers win her battle over cancer. I was grateful for any tools provided. I was so overwhelmed by my circumstances.

From that book I learned to be proactive. I learned about a man whose daughter had fought head and neck cancer and had beaten the odds. This helped me see that I was going to do my damndest to become a *living* statistic, a shining example. That book gave me a lot of resources to help me *fight* for my life. I was so grateful to my dear cousin for that gift.

Before that third surgery I literally felt out of control. It felt like I would never have control of my life again. I felt ruled by disease, darkness, bad luck and sadness. I also knew that this was the beginning, just the beginning. There was more to come. I anticipated more of this sadness and anger. I could see more of this darkness to come. I hadn't even reached the bottom.

I knew there was no way I could go peacefully into an operating room. The whole concept scared me to death. I asked the doctor if I could have a sedative, something to calm me down before they wheeled me into the operating room, strapped down in my gurney. That really helped. I was truly in La La land. I was probably singing ditties on the way into my operating room.

Once again, upon waking up from the third operation, my body was shaking uncontrollably. This time it happened four or five times as I reacted to the anesthesia that had accumulated in my system. I was in and out of consciousness. When I was conscious I was shaking. It was terrifying to be so out of control, to be writhing on the hospital bed.

The doctors came back. I was told that when they got into the surgical site, they found there was really not much of the area infected. After all that anxiety, anesthesia and another major operation, they had basically cut me open, looked in and sewn me back up. Dr. Costantino patted my shoulder and said, "One good thing about this ongoing infection is that it shows your body is actively fighting. We just need to get you healed up, so your head and neck can withstand the intense effects of your course of radiation. We must start it sooner rather than later to ensure any remaining cancer is killed."

A Place To Go

I duck away from familiar faces
My tears of first telling are too close
Time will heal the rawness
Where I go now
I go for my higher purpose
I am scared

<u>*Still*</u>

<u>*I go*</u>

I had to take on new ways of living and new ways of thinking of myself. After getting out of the hospital following my third surgery, I learned about Gilda's Club. It sounded like just the place for a lost soul like me. I felt a strong hunger for knowledge about my circumstances. It is a patient-run center for cancer survivors where the patients are the experts. I found I liked going there.

Gilda's Club was nicely set in New York City's West Village. Off New York City's renowned grid system the winding West Village streets are lined with old townhouses made of stone and brick. The neighborhood was full of vibrant NYC energy and attitude. I was able to walk the streets here. It was a good thing because I felt wild inside, like a scared caged animal.

I could lose myself in the sound and sights. I could just feel good and funky. The streets felt old and new at the same time. It is an uncomplicated place to be. In New York, it is okay to be different. Of course, it's better to be different and beautiful. It is still all right to walk the streets and feel okay, recognizing that you're not like everybody else. I would tell myself, "I am okay. I have a destination and I belong somewhere." I saw a woman wearing a T-shirt that read "F*** CANCER." I totally agreed.

Gilda's Club has a red door, a signature in the streets of the West Village. The red door leads to a warm, homey place. I felt better as soon as I entered. I felt comfortable, as if I could take refuge from the world.

I first went to an initial meeting where I had to introduce myself to others fighting cancer. During that meeting I felt on the verge of tears. I was the youngest. I was the most outwardly affected. I was the most obviously physically changed by the experience. I felt everyone else there could hide their scars. Their treatments could be tucked away. After chemo or radiation, they could simply live their lives where I was forever marked and changed, never to forget or overlook this time. I cried and I sobbed. I did not even want to speak, but I did.

I spurted out, "Hi, my name is Michele and I am a 33-year-old new mother. I was diagnosed with head and neck cancer. I sacrificed my right facial nerves in order to save my life." That was enough to shake me, but there was more I had to say. I forced myself to choke out, "I am here to say that I am not a statistic. I am in this to win it. I am going to fight." Then I bowed my head, hiding my face as I sobbed. I felt exposed. I was terrified to show my twisted face as these intense emotions played on my changed features. In that same moment I was fiercely proud that I had said what I had to say. I had made my claim among those who knew the weight of my words.

Gracefully You

Start to look at yourself with deep appreciation and reverence. You can make this a daily habit. As you brush your teeth, gaze lovingly into your eyes in the mirror. Look at yourself and tell yourself: *I love you, (insert your name).* Say it to over and over again. Really see yourself, acknowledge yourself, and value yourself.

This cherishing of you is the beginning of empowerment. You are one step closer to being full of self confidence and self love. As you practice this regularly you will begin to take it into your whole experience. Whenever you think of yourself, you will do so with love. Doesn't that feel good?

Gilda's Club offered cancer support groups. I could attend weekly meetings, hosted by a social worker and cancer patients. I understood that it was good to be around other cancer fighters. I decided it was something I would try on and see if it fit me.

When I arrived at my first meeting, my jaw almost dropped when I saw who would be my support. The youngest woman had to be 70 and they were all talking about the aches and pains of being old. I almost laughed as I excused myself as politely as I could and left immediately. Right then I did not want support from the very thing that I yearned to become, old. If I could accept any support, it would have to be from people of my own generation.

Although I never returned to that group, I did return to take Qi Gong and Yoga classes. They also offered speakers and wellness support groups. In addition, there was a resource library. I spent hours devouring every piece of available literature. I made every contact on the cork board. I was able to read about young women surviving. I was inspired.

One of my favorite things at Gilda's Club was their nighttime activities, like presentations by alternative medicine practitioners. I went to a presentation given by a medical doctor, Dr. Wendy, about energy healing. She was a highly educated MD. She opened a door to choice and empowerment.

She allowed me to begin to see things in a constructive way, one in which I could be a very active accountable participant. She gave energy readings to some of the audience. She read their chakras. I was enraptured. I wanted to know more about energy and how to access all the amazing power within me. She was in touch with some very powerful information and I was excited. I would make it play an active role in my healing.

Amazing Energy

East wind at my back pushing me forward
South wind sustaining me
West wind guiding me on the path going forward
North wind blowing inspiration from above

Feet on the ground head in the clouds
My hands reach into creation
I am divine
Life is divine
Thank you

Just after the third operation I found myself dead center in a bloody battle with head and neck cancer. It was a stark reality. The future was just a black void. A spiritual guide came to me in the form of an old friend, Simone. She and her mother had traveled hundreds of miles to spend an afternoon with me. During those few precious hours they relayed some seriously helpful life lessons.

Beautiful healing truths were literally brought to my door. I was lost and in a haze of shock and fear. I was numbed by prescription pain killers. The first thing they did was to let me know there was no judgment. Simone's mother said, "You will heal faster if you know that you are exactly where you should be. Try to let go of the what ifs and allow this experience to present its opportunities. Be open to the pain and uncertainty you feel."

I responded by saying, "But maybe this would not have happened if I had listened to my heart and taken a chance and changed my profession. I got addicted to the money."

Simone said, "You are judging yourself harshly. Judgment is never useful and generally is detrimental to healing. Your habitual behaviors have led you to the today you face. You cannot criticize yourself even when through the lens of healing you see that you created this illness through your past actions. Please, Michele, try not to judge yourself because it is a waste of precious time and energy."

This was difficult to do. I was filled with what-ifs, and how things might have been different. They basically hit me over the head with the *real* deal: I was where I was, period, and nothing would change that fact. By not judging and weighing myself through my old filters, I freed myself to heal. Simone and her mother helped. They lifted my eyes to the light of the universe of possibility. I was not here to judge. I was here to create.

They set a sacred space and we meditated. Simone led the meditation. She has a marvelous way of soothing. Her voice painted an amazing pathway to an inner sanctum. They reinforced that I was already whole, already healed. My soul had all the knowledge to make me perfect. In fact, I was perfect already.

When the meditation was complete both Simone and her mother commented on how strongly they felt the healing energies surrounding us. They left as quickly as they had arrived, but they taught me much that day. Just their presence in the room with me, helped me to know that they saw me and they still loved me. They did not judge me. I was acceptable just as I was. That simple truth was a beautiful and amazingly timely gift. In their eyes I saw the light of love, peace and prosperity. They made me realize that there was hope, and a universe full of possibilities. I discovered that sometimes opportunity is disguised as problems. I was able to digest it all because they allowed me to just listen gently. It felt like a refresher course. It was like I knew all of this already, but just needed a reminder.

That Which Breathes You

The energy that brings you into life is the energy that animates your body and keeps you functioning. Energy is the vital life force. In cultures of the East, it is known by different names: Qi, Chi, Prana. It distinguishes life from death. This energy nourishes the cells of your body. Energy has a structure within your physical body. For you to operate optimally your energy should flow freely. When energy gets blocked from moving throughout your energy anatomy it creates dis-ease. Dis-ease, if not addressed and its cause removed, can lead to disease. Much dis-ease is caused by stress. Stress has many forms: stuffed unexpressed emotions, old unforgiven wounds, self-deprecating inner dialogue, deep abiding anger, subjugation of your feelings to everyone else's. These are only some of the typical culprits that lead to blocked energy.

You can begin going in a new direction. You are the one who can make all the difference. Rediscover the power of your focus. You have a choice: you can choose to hurt or heal your body by the way you speak to yourself and how you see yourself. Trust that somewhere within you, you are already whole, already healed. Know this. Stake your claim; you have a right to health. The first step is to stop being so hard on yourself. You have done the best you could with what you had. Now you have options and you know it.

For me, it broke down into something like this: I was where I was and there was no going back. There was only going forward and that was just right. I now to understood that I had the power to create my future. That was what I had to do. I had created a self-perception that I was selling myself for a high paycheck. I had been putting on a suit and smothering my creativity. My compassion had been crushed. Through this veil I cloaked my mind in false stories for so long that it created a physical sickness in order to be heard. Now I was to heal myself and put balance into my life.

The "how" was up to me. I was the only one who could create a happy ending to this saga. I was the one who had the power to heal myself. I had to start where I was and recreate my life. I was terribly wounded and looked a fright. I did not recognize myself in the mirror. I was grotesquely swollen and one side of my face was slack and stared unblinking. It frowned back at me. I was twisted both inside and out. Forever marked, from this moment forward, nothing would ever be the same.

I looked around. I began to see truth in that no one is perfect. This facial paralysis brought my imperfections to the forefront for the world to see. From this one blow I was given the opportunity to start again. The power of energy made me giddy with excitement. All of a sudden I had tremendous resources.

I was raw when I began working with energy. I read avidly and research became a full-time undertaking. I studied energy, healing, mind-body medicine, complementary alternative medicine, whole-body medicine, spirituality, and anything else that I thought might help me. I deeply read many great authors from Chopra to Dyer, Hay to Myss, Siegel to Gerber, Abraham to Hill. I learned and applied their wonderful teachings.

Energy is the vital life force. It is that subtle something that electrifies this world. My energy has an anatomy within my body. My goal became to make my body my friend, not my enemy. I had to be sure that everything it was doing, it was doing with love. There are energy centers. These hubs of power keep my energy flowing through my physical body and out to the environment. I really dug the idea of making sure good vibes flowed freely in my space. This learning felt warm and familiar, like coming home to sweet comfort.

Disruption to my flow of energy was caused by stress in its many forms including how I visualized myself. I had kept up an internal dialogue of continually punishing myself for not achieving some impossible standards. Those habits, thoughtlessly created in my childhood, now ruled my days.

But they were no longer serving my highest good. Energy is also disrupted by physical injury or unexpressed emotions stuffed away and left to decay.

I began to see an energy therapist I had met at a presentation at Gilda's Club. I felt a void. I was in need of tools. I needed the equipment to become the warrior woman within. I became a sponge. I listened and learned. Using these new tools, I began heading in a new direction. I was the only one who could make all the necessary changes. I discovered my power was in my focus. I found that my thoughts held energy. I had a choice. I could choose to heal my body by the way I spoke to myself and saw myself. My tool set became the path of the chakras, the strength of vision, the healing of body, the gift of universal connection, the chance to impact tangibly from within to without. Somehow I knew and trusted I was already whole, already healed. I claimed my right to health.

I needed to stop being so hard on myself. Dr. Wendy explained that my chakras were not balanced. My heart chakra was completely open as if to say to the world, "Come on in and trample on me with your cleats." I had not protected my heart energy center. Therefore my energy was not flowing well through my heart energy center. Loss issues stem from fear of loss of love, safety, or even life. I had stored loss issues in my energy centers. Being afraid to lose, I could not afford to say "no" so everyone got my "yes," or my smile. I had never learned to say "no." I gave myself away without thought to the consequences. I needed balance. I needed to give expression to each of my energy centers.

Build Your Energetic Muscles And Help Free Yourself

Your energy centers each hold a primary truth to equip you to use the power of your free will. Take these truths gently into your consciousness and allow for their possibility. At the root of your energy structure, appreciate that you have a right to life. You are here, that is proof enough.

If you stop and realize that right this moment you are supported by something. It manifests in the physical world as a chair or floor. You are connected to and supported by the Earth, without even having to ask.

Continued on next page…

...continued from previous page

Understand that you are deserving. Know that you have the ability and the right to create and honor yourself. You have an inherent right to your personal power. You are permitted the expression of your unique personal identity. Give yourself the amazing gift of a deep abiding self love. Share your love with others, live with compassion. Trust in your inner knowing and you will go far.

I began to call my spirit back from all of the people in my past. I asked for it to come and be wholly present in me. My spirit was scattered to the winds because I had always responded to anyone's call. If no one called, I was sure to call them. I had a need to be needed. Now I was completely free to break away, to go within and be reborn. I was leaking from the head, for goodness' sake, what else was I to do? I was not one to sit back and become addicted to pain killers. That would have been the easy way. I had to find a better way. I was made for joy.

As a part of my healing process, I had to say goodbye to my facial nerve several times. This was because of the abrupt way it had been sacrificed. I had yet to accept the face reflected in the mirror. I was mourning the loss of it, but I was afraid to cry out. My life was broken. I could not smile it away. There was no covering my wound. I thought it was better not to feel the pain. It was too deep. I convinced myself to just get on with the stuff of living. This twisted face was my reality now, so I had to keep going. The depth of the pain in losing my smile was infinitely more than could be shed in a short time.

I was posed a question by Dr. Wendy: "If I lived but never interacted with anyone, would I have worth?" Seeking the answer was a wonderful unveiling of truth for me. I did not immediately answer. I needed clarification: did I do anything in life? Did I create anything? Nothing? Back to the question: was I still valuable in doing nothing? I resisted. How could one be valuable doing nothing? The wonderful simplicity of this truth astounded me. I was like a distant star. I was worthy. I was created. Therefore I was valuable, end of story. I did not need to *do* anything, I had nothing to prove.

Another early truth rediscovered, was intention. I was from the source of all things. In fact, that source is me. I have the power to create. I am the creator of my reality. With every thought and inner dialogue that I have with myself, I manifest my reality. To utilize my intention, I had to first uncover what inspired me. What did I desire? What did I want? To heal, I needed to fall in love with my life. I needed to reacquaint myself with my desires. I had to create a life direction that I could aspire to. The slate was clean, wiped clear of any past medals of honor and get-out-of-jail free passes. I took every opportunity to say, "Source, that I am, I intend this to be…" I needed to use intention to define my reality with laser-like focus. I would let nothing stand in the way of my seeing beauty in my life. My life could be made from what I decided to focus on, not what was thrust upon me.

I fell in love with a relatively new science: quantum physics. It was gratifying to find all of my intuition scientifically proven—energy was making itself known. I found an amazing quantum physics study that I shared with anyone who would listen. The study showed that a particle could be in two different forms at the same time: as a particle and as a wave, until it was observed. Then it became material in the form in which the observer decided he saw it. The reality did not come first, the thought came first. My friend Simone would say, "First came the word." Equipped with this knowledge I asked myself: "What shall I intend? What forms shall I make with such amazing powers of intention? What shall I create? This disfigurement will not define who I am."

Odd One Out

Step into the future baby
Step into the future baby
Step on in I said step on in
Step into the future
I'm gonna do it one step at a time
I'm gonna do it, baby, one step at a time

I went to some therapy sessions, and I really enjoyed my therapist's view of me. She saw me as a woman with chutzpa and strength. I told her I was afraid to go back to work. I could see myself breaking down anytime anyone did a double take or stared too long. She said, "Why don't you have a little script ready? You know: 'My name is Michele Howe Clarke and I had head and neck cancer. They removed my facial nerve and now my face is paralyzed. And how are you?'" I stared at her slightly aghast, thinking, *Hey lady I think that is Z and I am only at A, the freakin' beginning of the alphabet of healing. I am not ready to recite a damn script to anyone.* The disconnect from where I stood to the advice she gave was too great for me to cross at that time. Our sessions wound down after that.

During that time I sought out head and neck cancer support groups: anything that might help me deal better. I was excited to learn from a visit to my surgeon's office that a woman who suffered from facial paralysis was leading a facial paralysis support group. I needed help to learn how to cope with such an amazing change: of not being able to smile, of losing all normal appearance, of losing that familiar face in the mirror. Without having my friendly face I realized I had really lost something. It was something very substantial and it had sustained me through life. I left countless messages for this support group but never received a call back. I was angered because they should have taken their brochures out of doctors' offices where desperate people, like me, might be given false hope. One day the brochures disappeared. I was glad no one else would have my sad experience.

I went to a free cancer support therapist. During the first session, my assigned therapist was a young woman fresh out of training. During our one and only session, she just looked at me and said with such big eyes "I understand, you have every right to feel this way and, wow, this is hard." That was not what I needed. I needed her to ask pointed and direct questions such as: How are you going to go on? What are you going to do to feel good about yourself? What are you going to do to fall in love with yourself again? How are you going to kick this cancer's ass?

There were other such therapy missteps. I kept looking to find the support I needed. I found a young, 30-somethings cancer support group. I thought: *Okay, here is something I think I can commit to.* I knew I needed more help to deal with the harshness of my reality so I could continue to heal.

I met with the therapist who led the group and earnestly told her about myself. She said, "Wow, whoa, that must be really hard; a support group would be useful. But I should warn you that you will be the only one there dealing with head and neck cancer. It is so serious and rare, especially for one so young. Also, you will be alone in dealing with such a severe disfigurement. You are the most impacted and the others probably won't feel the depth of what you're going through. This is a group of mostly single people who will be more focused on getting back into their lives and into the dating scene again."

Great way to get someone to join your support group, lady, I thought. I was shocked, and saddened, to be so far removed from the support resources available. I was so upset that I cried until my insides hurt. Was there no support for me? I felt alone, adrift in a vast sea.

In that moment I vowed to myself that the support I needed would find its way to me. I gave it over and got out of my own way. After a damn good cry (or 100), I opened the doors of my faith and set myself free. I found much power in intention and I began to use it liberally.

Intention

Intention is a moving toward. By practicing intention you actually start moving toward your desires by harnessing thought and intending your desires to be. It is very simple to intend. Start by creating a mental picture of your desire. See yourself acting as if it has already happened. Then state: *I intend that I am_____ .*

State your intentions out loud, boldly. Listen to yourself making the intention with faith and have conviction it will be. Ask for your heart's desire; the sky is the limit. Ask that it come freely, effortlessly and easily by finishing your intention with "So be it and so it is."

Gratitude enhances the intention process. As you recognize that your intentions have come true, say "thank you" and know "so be it, so it is." Develop trust by consistently intending your desires. Then, believing and watching as they manifest into reality. Always remember to say "thank you" when they arrive. Over time you will notice that your trust turns into knowing that you can manifest your desires.

Preparing To Be Fried

Awake
The reality still here
CANCER
A mortality rising
Not a Statistic
The power of one
Successful Spirit
Life's joy
In every breath

Radiation steadily approached though I was still fighting the infection they said wasn't there, even after they cut me open to have a closer look. I chose to believe I would get well. I became the captain of my health-care team. I knew my thoughts manifested themselves in my body. I tried to keep them positive and tried to ask constructive questions. I remembered to love myself and care for me. The voice of my mother rang in my ears. I could hear her telling me as a depressed 15-year-old, "Michie, do you know yourself? That is your first job. You cannot love, trust or care for anyone else until you do this first for yourself." I kept my thoughts on the possibilities and not the statistics. I considered radiation to be a test like none I had taken before. I decided I would be strong, centered and positive.

I had six weeks to heal and get ready for my course of radiation following my third operation. This was the next amazing chapter in this saga of healing that lasted for many months. I had six weeks to find a place in my heart to be strong. I needed to be prepared to withstand an eight week course of radiation where I would go five days a week. I was warned of what to expect. I would become fatigued and have very little energy to do much of anything. I would have dry mouth. Open sores would develop in my mouth. My face would become extremely red and painful.

During my extensive radiation treatment, thick mucus would form. I would lose my sense of taste, and experience pain while eating. I would be chronically fatigued. My skin would feel like I had severe sunburn. I would lose movement in my mouth and my neck. I could experience depression. A time might come that I would have so much pain in my throat and mouth that I would be unable to eat.

There were other possibilities that the doctors would explain if they arose. The Western medical approach toward patient understanding is to give us just enough information to understand the basics. All other details will be explained if and when they come up. Essentially, I was on a "need to know" basis. It has been said that dying is the easy part, the hard part is living. I knew then that I could actually die and that I just might die sooner rather than later. The good news was I had a wonderful radiation oncologist Dr. Kenneth Hu who also spoke the language of hope with profound sincerity.

The first radiation session was a mock-up. The technicians custom made all my radiation accoutrements. I was tattooed on both sides of my face to make sure I was in the same exact position every day. They made a plaster cast of my face in order to fashion a hard plastic mesh face mask. This mesh mask would ensure that I could not move a millimeter for upwards of 30 minutes at a time. I would have to lie down on a steel table and be strapped down. Then this mask, with me in it, would be bolted into the table.

Radiation began the next day. During this treatment, radiation would build up in my body, causing all of its minor injuries to compound into serious pain. *Great,* I thought, *let the games begin.* Then I cried and cried, choosing to be honest with my feelings. The tears ran hot down my cheeks. I feared the unknown. I knew I had to find a plan to deal with the radiation.

The first heart-stopping fear was that I would be strapped down, literally bolted to a table for about half an hour five days a week. What was I going to do to keep my control when physically it was taken away? I knew instinctively, no one could control my mind or spirit. I would make this time an opportunity to stretch my spiritual powers.

I started my daily radiation practice by silently greeting the radiation machine. I kindly asked it to help me kill the cancer cells. I would lie on the cold steel table and give myself over to the process. I would accept my mask's tight embrace. I asked humbly for healing energy to be present and help me stay connected to "the source" of all things.

Every day for almost a whole summer, I was strapped to a radiation table, my face bolted onto it through a plastic mask. The mask had a scary resemblance to that murderer Jason from the horror movie. My facial flesh was so swollen it oozed through the mesh of the mask adding to the freakishness. Sometimes in this time of confinement, I had panic attacks. I would lose control of my focus and let in the reality of being strapped down and bolted to a table. I felt caught in a scene from another horror movie, *Hell Raiser.* All of my angst and fear would cause adrenalin to come rushing in, triggering my fight-or-flight reflex.

I could not escape. I had to bear down and go through this white fiery agony. Sometimes my mind hovered on the edge of an abyss. I thought I would go crazy, just break and shatter into a million pieces. In these moments my heart pounded so loudly it sounded like a drum. I couldn't help but hear its call. As the burning need to flee raced through me, I would stop time and listen to my heart's ancient song. It soothed me, lulled me, and held me in its loving embrace.

Strengthened by my heart's song, I breathed deeply through my diaphragm, filling up with oxygen, and goodness provided freely to all. I was grateful for my ability to breathe. I would look inside myself and comb my body with light. I would visualize a golden comb moving through each part of me, cleaning it of toxins and replacing it with warm glowing light. I mindfully watched my breath, watching it go in and out. I followed my breath through my body as it gave life sustaining oxygen to all its parts.

Sweet Breath

Breath helps in all things. Deep diaphragmatic breathing is a great way to connect in the moment. You can follow the breath on its journey through your body. See it entering your nose, moving down your throat into your belly, going deep in your lungs. It is feeding your body the stuff of life, nourishing you, and healing you. Watch it leave, taking with it all the stress, disease and fear with it.

For an immediate calming relief it helps to place the tip of your tongue to the top ridge of the mouth as you breathe in and out of your nose. When you are overwhelmed, take a moment to sit with your breath. Allow this practice to open the door to your graceful peace.

Again I asked my spirit to return from all the people and places of the past and become present with me, whole. I asked my organs to vibrate in perfect health. I visualized myself in my peaceful surroundings, sitting under a waterfall by a small pool, the water cascading warm and nurturing over my skin. The rock bed cradled me with its smoothness. The sun felt warm on my face. I aligned my energy centers and breathed through each one, a golden light spinning clockwise. I relaxed all parts of my body starting with my feet, asking each to be perfect.

Every day I would greet the radiation machine and say, "Hello machine. Are you ready to fight some f*** cancer today?" I felt camaraderie with the machine. I held a firm belief that the machine and I would force the toxins and cancer right out of me. I dubbed it 600 after the series number. When I was held by 600 and we did our work together, I spent time redefining my focus, understanding my intent, rebirthing my desires.

There was nothing but that moment. Being strapped down, unable to move, I discovered there was more to know than the materialism of the physical world. During radiation, I was able to take flight to the inner sanctum of myself where all things were possible. I operated under the premise that it would not do to waste time worrying about the future. This might be my only time. I contemplated the quantum physics theory that we are all different vibrations of the same types of string energy and the fascinating possibility of parallel realities.

Radiation was very difficult. We thought we might be able to have friends take care of Sage, giving Dwayne and I the ability to go to the treatments without her. It turned out that we went to radiation together as a family. Dwayne and Sage would sit in the waiting room. Of course Sage was just a breath of fresh air. Everyone in that waiting room had cancer or was related to someone who did. I saw some people fighting and not winning. I saw some people fighting cancer for the third time. I saw some people who were not even taking it on, they were just there. Some people completed their full course of radiation and some did not.

Many times, as the radiation ran its course, my face was so swollen that the technicians had to use their body weight to push down on the mask in order to bolt me to the table. The flesh of my face would pop through the openings in the mesh, straining for room to fit in the confined space. As if all of this wasn't difficult enough I had to walk around in public for the next hour after radiation with a mesh imprint on my face.

I was on this table in this motionless position for anywhere from 30 minutes to what seemed like several hours on more than one occasion. Sometimes, as all machines do, the 600 would break down. The techs would keep me on the table because it is not good to start and stop a treatment. Sometimes in these moments I had panic attacks. I experienced the edges of my world cracking, fracturing under such immense pressure. A cold sweat chilled me as I lost control of my constructive focus.

The shocking reality of being bolted to a table like a raving lunatic would hit me. My mind hovered on the edge of oblivion. I felt caught in a scene from my personal horror movie. All of my angst and fear would cause adrenalin to come rushing in. I would call out beseeching to be released from the burning agony.

One day Dwayne commented on the drastic dichotomy of our daily situation. We would drive into Union Square, the meeting place of all NYC's Villages—a vibrant crossroads full of youth and beauty. We would pass all of this life on our way down into the bowels of the city to the windowless basement of the medical clinic where the harmful rays of radiation were housed.

In the morgue-like environment of the radiation waiting room, we would sit together daily. The room was filled with patients and their wide-eyed relatives. The atmosphere was one of people torn from their lives and thrust into shock. They sat unblinking, staring in quiet bewilderment.

When we emerged from below each day we would try to do something family-oriented and life-affirming with our daughter, such as eat a picnic lunch in Union Square Park. Even though I looked like a mesh–imprinted, swollen-faced freak, we found love and even laughter in those days.

I completed my full course of radiation—every grueling session. I went every day and let it be what it was. It knocked the shit out of me. I moved through it somewhat dazed. My face carried a huge reddish purple mark from the intense radiation waves. I fought hard but it was an uphill battle. The radiation got to me. I was overwhelmingly fatigued. I had open sores and blisters in my mouth. My mouth would get so dry it would feel like a desert on fire as the radiation burned me from the inside out. I got to the point where I could not even swallow.

Better Yet?

Hurry up
And
Get well already

The radiation opened up my infection site. During the last half of treatment, I went everywhere with a bandage around my head. My infection began to rear its ugly head. A fissure, a perfectly round hole made from the inside out. It opened up in the middle of my ear and oozed green puss like some sick grotesque natural spring. The infection needed a way out. My body had created a new passage. Again, I walked around with what looked like two ear holes on one side. This was unbelievably shocking. *Would there be no end to the horror?*

This led to a new round of IV antibiotics. I learned I would have to be on these antibiotics for some time. This required that they be administered at home through a shunt implanted in a main vein. The shunt would be inserted in another surgery. I was trembling in the doctor's office and when I got out I started to cry and could not stop. Sobs wracked my body as I whimpered, "I can't take it anymore, Dwayne! When does it end?" I felt so overwhelmed, so utterly out of control. How many months would I be tortured with illness and fatigue?

"It will end when it ends. This is our new reality. You have to deal. They are only prescribing this to help," Dwayne said. I could tell that he was just plain sick and tired. His patience was hanging by a thread.

I could not stop crying and bemoaning my fate. I wanted to just fall to my knees and cry out, "Why me?" Dwayne was up to his ears in illness, stress and worries. He was there, too, dealing with all that we had been through, slugging it out everyday. I could practically see the steam rising from his head, and then he just snapped. He said, "That's enough, Michele, this is how it is. The doctors are not out to get you! They are trying to fight for your life. Deal with it!" His voice was full of the same frustrated rage as mine.

I ranted, "You don't understand. I have a right to be weak and feel sorry for myself once in a while." Dwayne had had it. "No, you don't! You have a daughter," he said. He stopped the car, and then calmly stated, "I am going home, Michele. You go to the infectious disease doctor alone." He let me and Sage out on the side of the street. I was sobbing and shaking.

I called my sister Nikki as was my habit when I was down. I knew I could tell her everything and she would just be there to listen. "Nikki," I said, "Dwayne just blew up and left. Now I have to go to the infectious disease doctor alone and I have Sage with me." I was crying hard. "I'm a mess, I'm sick of this shit. I feel like I am breaking." Nikki did as she always does—just listened and didn't try to solve the problem.

"I know, Miche, this is a bitch." Her voice broke as she began to cry with me. Having Nikki as a sympathetic ear gave me the strength to get myself together. I picked myself up off the Mid-town Manhattan corner and stepped toward the positive.

"Okay, Nikki, so I am neck deep in this. I try to convince others not to pity me and to believe I will come out of this winning. But I have never felt so beat up. I need to live in self love. I claim my life back. I claim my vibrancy. I claim my beauty. I claim my laughter. I redefine my smile. I value me and fall in love," I said. I was feeling able again. Nikki laughed through her tears, "That's right, Miche, you got this."

Your Preference

Your personal preferences are what make you a unique individual. Pay close attention to the areas of your life that cause you unhappiness. In your dissatisfaction, you are presented with an opportunity for illumination. Through dissatisfaction you are forced to define what your preferences are. By aligning your thoughts and thereby your feelings with it, you have the power to draw your aspirations to you.

As you move through life you must define your preferences again and again as you reach new vantage points. When you attain a long-held desire, you will need a moment to enjoy your new view. Allow yourself to embrace the experience of an aspiration made real by the power of choice. Sooner rather than later, life's natural tendency toward dissatisfaction will lead you to define your next set of preferences.

Once you have a desire stirring and you feel that sweet sense of hope, your preferences will become more precise. There is an old Indian saying, "the path is the goal." As you get better and better at defining your preference and aligning your thoughts with it, you will begin to enjoy your path more and more as it begins to unfold to your liking.

Feel better by choice; you are becoming a master framer of your life. Your primary power in this life is your point of focus. It is your choice how you interpret this life, how you tell yourself your story. The opportunity is on and it's all up to you. You control your focus.

You're in the driver's seat; you can decide where to direct your life. Your life really is the result of your preferences. Start using your power of choice. Add choice points throughout the day. Whenever you feel stressed or catch yourself running a negative tape, flip the script. You can now pause, catch yourself, and realize you have the power to choose a better now. Give yourself the gift of choice. Get giddy, quick.

I went to the infectious disease doctor's office alone with my infant daughter. Anyone who looked could tell that I had been crying, a lot. Sage being there made it somehow okay. Sage was so beautiful and new, she simply brought joy to everyone she met. She has these large knowing eyes that shine on people. She makes you feel warm and fuzzy. I just sat back and watched in awe as she spread her magic. I could not help feeling better. I took a cab home only to find Dwayne not there. I called him and found that he was still in the city. He was waiting for me to call so he could pick us up. That made me giggle a little. He really is a love.

That night I wrote my father a letter.

Dear Dad,

I miss you. I know you are close. Can you believe this is happening to your daughter? I don't know where I am in all this. I am not communicating well. I am scared. I get upset when I look in the mirror. This is my one shot. How do I go on? How can I wait and see? How do I live through this?

Dwayne and I are working through it each day. I know he is under a lot of pressure and trying to deal. It is hard, I used to take care of so much and now I need so much care.

Dad, I want to shock myself out of this numb detachment. To be the person I know I am. I have lost the thread of how to make a wish a reality. I need to study the art of living.

Thanks for listening, Dad. I know I can do it, I am capable. I resound in myself, I feel myself changing. I move forward into a new chapter. I choose excitement; I am always up for a challenge.

xoxoxox - Miche

I had five days of radiation left with anywhere from two to six weeks of antibiotics at home. It took about four hours to administer the IV twice a day. I had to sit still because I was attached to a wall where the IV bag was hung. I felt this was a set back because I was so tired and nauseous. I had no sense of taste; everything tasted like rubber. Not that it mattered because

I had trouble swallowing. The radiation had made my throat a raw, pulpy, painful mess.

I went way uptown to a new hospital near Columbia University to have the shunt put into my arm for the IV antibiotics. I changed into my blue paper gown. Again, Sage and Dwayne were by my side, but as always I went into surgery alone. No anesthesia to put me out for this one. I was awake for the whole thing. A young, tall, man entered and greeted me jovially. I immediately learned what I suspected when he walked in: he was yet another cocky Physician's Assistant. He had trouble finding a good vein. This was nothing new. He got more and more frustrated with his lack of success. I asked him, "Could we take a break?" He replied, "You should get used to this. This is your life now." *Ugh,* I thought.

Working It Through

A Place For Me
Oh bring me to a place in the sun
Where spirits never grow old
Even though bodies do
Show me the way to a place
Where I am welcomed with a
Glad smile and uncorrupted thoughts
A place where emotions are given freely
Without the hindrances of pride, greed or motives
A place where I can be one
With people such as these
Oh, this is the place for me
So let me find it or make it
Somewhere in this ball of confusion

Over the next few weeks I did not move around much. I was exhausted. I would sit as still as a statue. I was a silent witness. I observed my environment with no judgment. I was present and aware. Sage blossomed before my eyes. She was amazing and such a shining reminder of the good in my life. I would watch her eating. She made these wonderful noises of satisfaction. Zion, our cockapoo, sat at attention by her feet, watching the food with pleading eyes. My daughter showed me wonder. I felt my heart expand.

For me, being such a "yes" person for all my life had caused me to feel that I had given myself away cheaply. I was last on my priority list; I had lost my own importance along the way. In the face of raging seas in my life, I needed myself more than ever before. Alone, I could float better out there in the depths, with Dwayne, my family and dear friends to buoy me. I began to close down to the curiosity seekers. I just stopped thinking and planning. I returned very few calls.

Instinctively I hunkered down and got ready to get through this, come hell or high water. I needed to close a lot of chapters of my life that were toxic and draining. These goodbyes were probably long overdue. Whatever the reason, it felt right for me to lighten up on my internal responsibility to please the world.

During the last weeks of radiation I learned to weather a storm. I just dealt moment to moment honestly. I asked my family to give me space. My feelings were so unformed and raw. I had to find my way back to myself and take ownership of the present. I needed time with no distractions, time to heal and lick my wounds. I had spent a lifetime being what I thought everyone else wanted. I decided not to worry about what others thought of me. It only mattered what I thought and how I thought it.

I owned my authentic "No," and declined many social invitations. I took myself away, as if I were across the sea, not available for small talk. I simply could not be reached easily and I was okay with that. This was how I was guided to my future through the very murky present. I answered only to the Source of me. Gone was my shot at superficial perfection. I had to live an authentic life. My mask was torn from me. I had lost my everyday suit of armor. I would overstand my situation, instead of just understanding it. I became the silent observer, the non-judgmental witness. Thereby granting myself a source of elevation as I detached from the outcome.

The Authentic You

Now it is vital that you be truly you; influenced only by you. You need to express yourself as you, by you and for you. No holds barred. Like so many of us, perhaps you were programmed early on to say "Yes" even when you would rather say "No." You feel guilty, as if you are letting people down just by saying "No." Yet, you continue to tie yourself up with obligations to other people. Do not forget the ultimate value of your time, the obligation you owe yourself to fully express your truth. It is of critical importance that you begin to say "Yes" when you mean yes and "No" when you mean no. By putting an end to selling your time so cheaply, you buy back your self-worth.

When I allowed myself to stay present, I could simply notice my inner gremlins yammering at me with to-do lists and all my insufficiencies. I looked at my options and even created new ones. I did not need to respond as I had for 33 years. I exercised my power and used my ability to create.

Right after getting out of the hospital from my second operation, I started to build my focus. I never wanted to feel that out of control again. I wanted to take control of all that I could. My mind was all in my domain. I began to read and study. I devoured books about mind-body medicine, wellness, complementary alternative medicine, nutrition, healing arts, energy, spirituality, energy centers, archetypes, visualization, prosperity, abundance, intention and love. I filled composition notebooks with my lessons and views on creating a fulfilling future. I met myself along the way and re-introduced myself. I started to integrate these new and powerful forces into my life. I still worried about the uncertainty of my future. I was afraid to think about what the PET, CT and MRI scans would tell every three months. My future was so cloudy. I constantly had to remind myself not to be in my head, thinking and worrying about the future. Life is made up of a series of todays. I knew that worry was a big waste of my precious time and energy. Negative thoughts could be detrimental to my life span.

Sage was now almost a year old. She was a little star—beautiful, interested and clever. When she looked at me I fell in love with the moment. Sage came along at a great time. I was able to savor the joys and trials of early motherhood, unspoiled by the cancer experience. When she was six months old the hard stuff of infancy was over. She was just there with those large knowing eyes that appropriately matched her name. It is ironic how things work sometimes. She was a gift to help us through this terrible, dark time.

I studied my life's creation. My choices had led me to where I stood, cancer and all. I saw myself clearly, all the little habits that placed me here. I was a worrier. My gremlin shone the light on the worst case scenarios, creating fears that did not really exist in the moment. I made lists and lists of things to do. I made everything a big deal and shouldered all the responsibility so I could see myself as a martyr.

Habit's Ponzi Scheme

Everyone is a victim of habit. Habit grows out of environment. The habits of early childhood cling to you throughout your life. Habit is created by repeatedly directing one or more of your five senses in a given direction. It is through this repetition principle—out of doing the same thing or thinking the same thoughts or repeating the same words over and over again—that a negative, or positive, habit is formed. Once a habit is formed it can be likened to a groove in a record and your mind like the needle that so easily fits in and seeks out that groove.

In truth, historically I was not coming from my power, nor standing up for myself. I had a hard time expressing myself authentically at work. I thought I was far too strange for these straight suits. All I did was grin and bear it, always hiding my clay feet. My winning smile and shining eyes bought me the money ticket. I felt empty. Money and drinking became my rewards. They had replaced the sources of true pleasure.

At any opportunity I would be sure to mention to all who would listen that, "I am only doing this for now. It is not what I will be forever." I was secretly ashamed to have sold out for the money, to have signed up so easily to being owned by a corporate paycheck. I acted as if investment banking was just my part-time gig, when I really bled for it. I was lying to myself, too absorbed in the pursuit of the Myth of Perfection. My reward came from the lure of security and outward appearances.

I had become a shell of myself. My job became the centerpiece of my life and my angst. I was the "Yes" person, even if it was the last thing I wanted to do. I was very successful but I was sure I did not deserve it. I obsessed about my imperfect size. I rode the merry-go-round of broken promises and better tomorrows for seven years. I was lost in that life. I filled my time with excess whether it was work, stress, consumption, or alcohol.

There is an energy theory that my cancer and subsequent deformity were caused by unexpressed energy blocking the flow of my chi. It is true; I did not love myself very well in those years before cancer. My self-love had many contingencies. It hinged mainly on the attainment of success. I constantly redefined success, setting it further and further away. I made sure I was never good enough.

When I looked in the mirror, I almost found beauty. However, there was always some flaw. Overall, I would "do" for now, until I could change this or that. I was not enough and never would be. Over the years I grew in size, mediocrity and self blame. I knew I did not feel my best but I kept numb by encasing myself in instant gratification. Liquor helped keep me pacified.

If asked, I would smile and say flippantly, "Yeah I'm doing well, but the irony is I do not deserve my success at work. I think I have fooled them all." I lived afraid to be myself. I feared if I did, then I would be discovered for the sham I believed I was. I was a party girl out to have fun. I definitely had my share. Now, playing for my life, I had to flip my limiting script, stand in my power and know that I was enough.

Be Present

The ego chatters endlessly, warning you against danger. The ego is simply a defense mechanism. The ego spends your life proving dangers are ever present. The ego cannot easily be at peace. Its sole purpose is protecting you. The ego's story is one based on fear. It constantly perceives threat. The ego is here to tell you everything that is wrong. It points out every scary thing in the big bad world. Nonetheless, please do not hate poor ego. In its purest form ego is here to protect you, to keep you alerted to danger.

Can you imagine what it would be like to be fully present, to simply see things for the infinite details of beauty that they are? When you get stuck in your mind, in your story, it separates you from the moment. You are unaware of what is really happening and all the possibilities available in this very moment. The goal-oriented mind is insatiable, its quest for answers never ends. You cannot think about this moment without moving away from the present but you can feel this moment and stay fully present.

Now, I worked on my energy. I liked the direction my life was taking. I owned my "No" and used it freely. I began to live authentically. I felt congruent with my spirit. I was still very emotional and raw. Some days I hurt as if knives were piercing me. I was not comfortable knowing I had to reveal my imperfection so blatantly for the rest of my life. I missed being able to hide my scars away and show a good face.

I did not want to be pitied and I did not want to go around crying in front of people. I focused on not reacting to events not of my making. I chose what to focus on in the moment. I had a constant reminder staring me in the face, to love myself and use my power to create my new life. I was ready. I had to be because the bridge was burned. There was no going back to my comfort zone. I faced the challenge. I let go of the Myth as it no longer served a purpose.

We're Not In Kansas Anymore

Who but me
Can make me smile
Askew, lopsided
Still I smile
Who but me
Can believe in more life
Scarred and hopeful
I move forward
Who but me
Can appreciate the love
Surrounded by care
I reach out
Who but me
Can

Going back to my life in Long Island City was a very difficult adjustment. This whole loss of normal appearance was a daily revelation for me. Every encounter held relevance. I began the process of cleaning out. Even seemingly minor acts held great significance—like cleaning out my vanity became a ritual to let go of yester-year. There was so much that I had accumulated that I no longer needed.

Returning to what was once normal was shocking for me and everyone around me. The people I used to walk my dog with were unsure how to react or speak to me. They acted as if they did not see me. I acted like I did not want to be seen. I walked my dog less and less. I had a big white bandage around my head and I looked warped. The tricky thing about my disfigurement is that my face becomes starkly twisted when I speak or show emotion. It made it more difficult for people to see my situation, especially those who knew me casually before. They couldn't help but silently compare the normal before to the distorted after.

I shuddered to think of myself in an elevator at my office. Hundreds of people who barely knew me passing by. All those people gawking and feeling sorry for me. I could just see myself bursting into tears. I was sick with the thought of it. It showed me how judgmental I was. All of my fears were just reflections of how I would have reacted to someone in my situation. How would I have acted if it had been some other poor son-of-a-bitch that I worked with? I would have been sure to mention it to Dwayne and any other person who might be interested. I could not imagine myself returning to a place where I had always made myself feel less than and not good enough. Especially not like this.

I had not been a big risk taker over the past eight years. I had gone after money and security. I was unhappy in my work but consumed by it. I felt unsure of myself, my knowledge and my skill. I thought I was faking it, so I carried this secret that slowly ate away at any confidence I might acquire. It was hard to swallow. I was this high earner surrounded by people, moving steadily up the career ladder, but I did not buy it for one second.

Memories brought tears these days, but only for as long as I allowed it. I reminded myself that I was more than a functioning face. However, life without a quick smile was proving shattering. Some days I just cried. I wanted to return to the past. I saw in clear 20/20 hindsight how good I had had it. Now, there was no denying something was wrong with me. One just had to look to see. Sometimes when I felt strong I would look at myself and think, *okay, now I am truly remarkable.*

The social butterfly had gone quiet. No more fluttering from here to there. No more contacting this or that person. No more making sure my social calendar stayed full. The whole bar scene was pretty much neutralized. There was no more easy banter. The quick smile, so easy before, now only revealed how disfigured I was.

I began a process of shutting down and slowing down. I was keenly aware that I could never shut down completely. At those very moments of deep despair, I felt the siren call of my vat of painkillers the first surgeion made sure were always on hand. When the pills called, "Take me. I'll make your pain go away." I would hear my beautiful baby, Sage, babbling as she discovered the world and say, "Hell no!"

I studied health. The pursuit of health led me to focus directly on my body. How I fueled it and the way I treated myself were of the utmost importance. I tried to eat more naturally. I consumed fewer packaged and prepared foods. I met a friend of mine, Paige, at Whole Foods in Chelsea on one of my shopping trips. She has a great ability to make me laugh. She is a very vibrant, street-savvy New Yorker who says it like it is. When she saw me she said, "Hey it's not so bad."

I said, "Well it is what it is."

"Yeah, well, some people were just born ugly," Paige retorted. I laughed out loud at her quick dry wit because it is true. *What is a face anyway?*

I knew then that what I needed was to graduate from relying solely on my smile. I needed to find the depth, and the source of me. I began to see that what made me was not my smile. Even though in the past that smile certainly helped to define me. In fact, it served as a major crutch, carrying me through many a trial.

It was the past showing its face that reminded me of the cruel twist mine had taken. Visits with old friends and family brought the past flooding to my door. I cried, railing inside, *Why me? What is this all about?* I felt a wave of grief and sadness. I missed of my old life. I missed my old face and my old piddly worries.

It was so hard to talk to friends and family. My social mask was completely ripped away. Experiencing emotion made my face twist. I did not want to be seen. It was other people who saw my face distort every time I spoke, smiled or laughed, not I. Sometimes I could be sweetly oblivious for a time. Then I would see myself in mid-expression and my breath would catch. My eyes would fill with tears. *That's me* I would think sadly.

My emotions swept through me, randomly triggered by varied events and people's reactions. I didn't feel like having everyone see me cry. I felt bitter at being exposed. *Would I ever feel normal again?* I doubted it. I tried to make sense of this. One thing's for sure, old habits die hard, even in the most dire situations. I looked in the mirror. I saw the imperfections, thinking, *today it's pimples, tomorrow inflammation, the next day redness.*

My relationships with people were changing fast. Sometimes the silence was deafening. From the beginning I did not want this or that person too close. I protected myself from judging eyes, eyes full of pity and comparison. People didn't know how to be with me, and I didn't want to have to explain. I wanted them to read me and get it. I wanted them to stand by but not get too close. I was angry that their lives continued on as before. I grieved for all I'd lost: my smile, my mortal innocence, control and my normalcy.

It made me crazy to think people would feel badly for me. It took my breath away to know that people would pity me and then count their blessings. I understood knowing about my circumstances would make many feel better about their own lives by comparison. It's human nature. It's what I would have done if I was not the poor son-of-a-bitch who was the object of their pity.

Dwayne worried about me because I was so quiet. He said, "I have to worry about your emotional well-being like I never had to before." I was trying to strip myself bare of the Myth of Perfection to learn that all is not as it appears. I still had a strong, chastising, negative voice habitually telling me what to do: lose weight, be active, eat healthy, keep friends, show face, stay in control, make lists, keep busy, strive for perfection, worry about the what ifs, and know you will never be enough.

I was sick to death of that nagging voice always finding fault. Now I wanted to believe in myself and trust myself to act consistently. I wanted to honor my body. I refocused. I became present and mindful of the process. I was alive therefore I had something to offer. *Boom, there it is!*

Listen to Your Heart

Your heart connects you to the pulse of Mother Nature and all of the subjects of her earthly realm. The sound of your heartbeat is the throb of life. In your heartbeat you can hear the primal rhythm of the drum all life beats to. When all else is chaos take a moment to center on the sound of your heart. It may take practice to still yourself enough that you can hear your heart speak. The fastest way to hear it quickly is to cover your ears, close your eyes and listen for it. When you hear its soothing beat you remember all that you are. In its gentle song you hear the voice of love and feel your connection to everything. Be still; listen to your heart. You'll find it has a lot to share with you.

If you listen to your heart you will discover what really gives meaning and purpose to your life. You can meditate on your heart and ask it for guidance. Ask what it needs and wants for you. Listen to its gentle song and commit yourself to getting fully involved in what inspires you. When you are energized and feeling good, recognize it. Take a moment to understand what it is that you are enjoying. Define what it is that energizes you. When you find yourself so pleasurably involved with something that you lose track of time, remember it and please, DO IT AGAIN. Aim to feel good. Make that happen by active choice.

The only way I could begin again was to remove myself from reminders of the past. I had to rebuild myself. I had to ask myself better questions: How can I make my life sweeter? How can I love myself more as I am now? How can I experience bliss daily? I became stronger, though the dark specter of fearful scenarios still haunted me.

I was altered and marked. I was touched and changed. But I was a warrior. I had a primal will to survive. I stopped trying so hard. I asked in meditation for help to *just be*. I started to focus on the process of my life. The daily routine I had hurried through to get on to the next thing was now precious. I became present. I stayed mindful of doing what I was doing. I was not planning in my head or talking to myself. I just kept breathing and focusing on the task at hand.

Feel Your Breath

An easy way to get present quickly is to follow your breath on its journey into and out of your body. As you focus on the feeling of breathing, be grateful for all that you have. See your breath nourishing the very cells of your body. Smell the fragrance in the air. Now focus on breathing in peace and breathing out toxins. Let your breath soothe you from the inside out.

It seemed to some of my close friends and family that I was shutting myself away. I knew what I was doing. I was removing my armor. I was readying myself to win my life. I was quiet, listening to my heartbeat. I heard it as a universal beating of nature, connecting me to everything. I focused on my heart and listened to anything it might have to share. I could feel that my heart appreciated my standing up for myself. I had to stay focused on what served me best now. I had to move toward my sense of meaning and purpose.

What was my dream? If I wasn't pursuing my dream, what *was* I pursuing? I accepted the fact that I was living that moment and no other moment existed. I allowed life to flow. I did not fight the current. I believed healing would come. I used my power of choice — I simply noticed that I had a choice. I had options in my every moment. I stayed in process. I gave myself the present of choice.

Dream It Up

Your imagination is the most amazing gift. The imagination is the workshop of the human mind, the creative power of this life. Create the qualities you seek in your imagination first and see yourself in possession of them. Your material achievements grow out of organized plans that you create in your imagination. First your imagination forms the thought. Then it organizes the thought into ideas and plans. Then you see the evidence of the transformation of those plans into reality.

Self-confidence is very important to success. Your thoughts either assist or undermine your efforts. Thought-by-thought you are creating your future. Let your goals become reality in your imagination first and never doubt their attainment. You receive as you believe, in other words, **Receive it** in your imagination first and then **Believe it**. Believe in yourself, first and foremost.

Get enthused! Enthusiasm is a state of mind when you are stimulated and inspired to act on your aim. You can become enthused by basking in your future success, really enjoy it. Your enthusiasm is a vital force that impels action. As you mix enthusiasm into your everyday pursuits, you stay energized. Enthusiasm urges you to put your knowledge into action. Become intoxicated on your enthusiasm. Visit us at www. faceforwardbook/tickettothrive.com to receive your free Goal Stroll and get psyched about your life.

You are the master of your life by the fact that you can control your own thoughts. With the aid of your focused thoughts, you can create whatever you desire. You need to guard your thoughts more carefully. The power to think as you wish is the only power over which you have absolute control. It is within your power to control your thoughts. Thus the responsibility rests squarely upon your shoulders whether your thoughts are positive or negative. Think thoughts of a positive, expectant nature and watch those thoughts create those prosperous conditions.

Back To Nature

Pointers

Don't let yourself be a man of flesh with a heart of stone
On your walk down the road of life do not step on the resting
Live your life. Don't let life live you.
Don't you see, you never fail until you stop trying?
This is your life. Don't be afraid to grasp your soul.

I felt a call to return to Sandy Hill, my country home in the endless mountains of Pennslyvania, for much of my healing. The landscape and natural setting greatly comforted me. As I sat in the high chi of the mountains I felt capable and in harmony with Mother Earth. A healing power hummed through me.

I had to ponder. I was still taking it all in. The change would only become more evident as time revealed the diminished parts of me. My mortal innocence stolen, I was no longer invincible. The sweet oblivion of my indulgent lifestyle was gone forever. Now there was a very real end and I would go to it alone.

With nature cradling me on all sides, I worried about nothing. I permitted myself to do nothing. I immersed myself in some of the main themes of healing and wellness. What I visualized impacted on how my body responded. I laughed whenever possible. Laughter is one of the greatest healing agents. Babies laugh hundreds of times a day. Adults laugh very little. I got outdoors and into nature. I forgave my bad days. There will always be those, we all hold both light and shadow.

I did Dr. Bernie Siegel proud and did not allow minor pains to become major symptoms nor did I allow myself to fall into the trap of worry. What I was living for became more and more apparent as I reacquainted myself with the source of me. I felt strong and decisive. I was determined to be healthy. I did not suppress my fear of dying. I faced it. I did not kid myself. I understood that I had a life-threatening disease that could kill me.

What You Want

If you are like most people, then you know more about what you do not want. People often do not know what they do want. They don't know what their heart yearns for. It is critical now to focus on what you desire. The easiest way to figure out what you do wish for is by how you feel. You should not feel neutral or lukewarm about a goal. You should be rather like a kid in a candy store yelling "YES, YES! I want THAT!" You are looking for that giddy flush of excitement. When you feel that, you know you are on to the thread of your aspiration.

Your reality is manifesting based on the vibration of your emotions. You are always creating vibrations that attract like vibrations. The way you create most effectively is by feeling good and thereby drawing a positive attraction. When you know what it is you want more than anything else, you can activate your attraction power. Figure out what you crave. Get really clear on it.

Here are some questions to get you started in the direction of naming your desire:

Continued on next page…

...continued from previous page

If you could change one thing about your life what would it be?

What do you want MORE of in your life?

If you knew there was no way you could fail, what would you go do right now?

What inspires you?

What's something you would love to do?

For your life to be wonderful, what would you need to change?

What's one way you could laugh more every day?

What are three of your greatest attributes?

What are you happy about now?

What are you anticipating?

Before cancer, the future was always clear and bright. Now I could not see myself in the future. That was scary. I could see Sage as she grew and Dwayne by her side, but I couldn't quite see me there in the future. I would say to myself as I walked out each day or did Qi Gong, *I am definitely on a unique journey. I now wear the markings of a warrior. I am enough. I love myself wholly. I trust myself. I am greater than the flesh. I am more than my face.*

Dwayne worried when I got quiet. He would ask, "Michele, are you okay?"

I would look at him and say, "Yes, I'm okay. Are you okay?"

"I'm okay, if you're okay," he would reply. I hoped he was staying because he wanted to. It was scary to want to be desired as I was before. Was it practical? Was it even possible? I asked Dwayne, "When you look at me, do you think I am still beautiful?" Dwayne said, "Honey, only 1% of you is changed. It just happens to be the 1% that is most visible. What am I supposed to do, trade you in for a new model? I love you."

So It Is

Your subconscious mind can be controlled and directed by your conscious (voluntary) mind, but not through sheer will. Any thought which is held in your mind, repetitiously, has a tendency to direct your physical body to transform the concept into its material equivalent. Concentration is the key to this process. To bring the material representation of your intention into reality it must be backed with a persistence that knows no defeat until it is taken over by your subconscious mind.

The subconscious mind accepts and acts upon all information that reaches it whether it is constructive or destructive. The subconscious mind does not know whether the information comes from the outside, from your own conscious mind or an external source. Desire is the seed of all achievement. Stimulate your mind with a strong, deeply-seated desire so that the powers of your mind will function constructively.

Select your primary aspiration. Fix your conscious mind upon thinking about what you want with enthusiasm. This will consistently train it to seek the positive. Your enthusiasm then influences your subconscious mind to develop the blueprint to attaining the physical reality. You now have a compass to use to actively navigate. The way may not open suddenly, fully formed. It may open slowly instead, only one step at a time.

Therefore, when you are conscious of an opportunity, take the initial step without hesitation. Do the same with all the subsequent steps. Decision is essential for the attainment of your goals. As you practice this more and more, you will develop faith and trust in the process. That confidence will increase the efficiency of your manifesting. Continuous and intense faith is a key ingredient in keeping your objective engaged. Remember to keep your mind in a confident state of enthusiastic expectancy of attaining your goal. You must keep this focus at the forefront of your mind until it becomes real and authentic for you.

Words hold so much power. Words can have a positive or negative effect. Delete powerless words from your language. Do not *try*, or *hope*, or *want*. Instead *intend* and *be*. Start saying, "I intend that…" and "I am…"

I had time on my hands, time like I never knew existed. I had seemingly infinite do-nothing days on the horizon. In the silence of the mountains I listened to my inner stirrings. Neither my time nor my mind was being loaned out on business. I was, for the first time in my life, in full control of the direction of my mind and my day.

I walked through the woods and across the fields, no matter how short the walk or how tired I was. I made sure to commune with nature each day. I appreciated nature's bounty—an amazing rock large enough for two to sit on faced an apple tree, big fluffy white snowflakes floated from the sky on frosty wind. I felt blessed to have the time to sit on a rock facing an apple tree that still held fruit and greenish leaves. The last vestiges of autumn amidst a landscape of white. All the surrounding trees stood stark and barren, swaying in the wind.

I connected with my inner Source. It was just beyond the daily dialogue, the to do lists, the deadlines and the pleasant distractions. Guidance sat in the inner silence, available anytime. My spirit sang with possibilities. I was well in the mountains, surrounded by nature.

This was how I was guided to my future through the very rocky present. I answered only to the Source of me. My shot at perfection was gone. I now had to live an authentic life. My smile was torn from me. I had lost my armor and my admission ticket to the pursuit of the Myth of Perfection.

I went to a reunion of friends. These beautiful women who travelled far to support me. Paige, Felicia, Jane and Sarah were buoys. They brought me light and love. They helped me remember that there had been good times. They helped me believe there would be more to come. My excellent friend Jane hosted the gathering in my honor. Her wonderful Truro Cape Cod home was situated on the banks of an inlet river which ebbed and flowed with the tide. We walked in the river bed during the day and watched it become a deep river at night.

Our previous times together were habitually centered on socially-lubricating alcohol. Historically, I was the social-drinking ringleader, always ensuring that alcohol was present. These women did not know me without a drink in my hand. Times and our situations had changed, but this was still an ingrained routine we had always followed. With that routine in place, we laughed, talked sincerely and moved together as a pack through the streets and docks of Wellfleet, Massachusetts.

During that time I had a big bandage around my head. The hole near my ear continued leaking. The fissure was not healing. The radiation had beaten down all healing strength as it fought to kill the malignant cancer cells. There was a moment when we were all sitting around a table lit by candles in the night air on the deck. I suddenly felt that the light was shining a hundred times brighter on me than on the others. I felt flawed and totally exposed. I abruptly moved my chair until I was once again sitting in the shadows, soothed by dark cover.

I understood my behavior and made allowance for my reticence. It was important for me to accept my shadow. It will walk with me all the days of my life. I did not excuse myself. I did not apologize my perception away.

Exceptional Me

Enter the circle
Give what you have to give
Take what you need
The circle lies in you
(A song we sang at the ECaP Retreat)

After that reunion and in the middle of the lingering infection, I went to an ECaP retreat. ECaP stands for Exceptional Cancer Patients, founded by Dr. Bernie Siegel. ECaP is headed up by Dr. Barry Bittman. It was held in the far reaches of western Pennsylvania.

The reason I traveled so far with a leaking head, all bandaged up, is best summarized by this ECaP statement:

"Our mission is to provide exceptional resources that help people facing the challenges of cancer and other chronic illnesses discover their inner healing resources. Based upon the science of mind-body-spirit medicine. We celebrate every person's potential for rediscovering wholeness, balance and inner peace."

It really was an amazing experience. Dwayne and I were there with about 15 other couples who came from as far away as Germany, Canada, and California. All of us were fighting a serious battle with cancer. Our very lives were at stake. We came together to heal. In the words of ECaP, "Healing is putting back into your life what has been missing." I found this philosophy so inspirational—such a wonderful way to look at sickness and healing.

I missed many things during the eight years I worked as an investment banker. I had put away my spiritual practices, all my soul work, and hung it all up for a big paycheck. I proved to myself that I could achieve any goal through sheer force of will and sacrifice. I could rise from a lowly analyst to vice president in one of the most coveted careers in the financial world. I did it and gave an extraordinary performance, but I always felt hollow. I felt as if I was being filled up with other people's shit and other people's personas. I put on this uniform everyday to become something that I wasn't. My soul was left at home crying, begging to be let out.

There was a Jacuzzi at the hotel where the ECaP retreat was being held. After one of the evening sessions, Dwayne and I went into the Jacuzzi. There was another cancer fighter there from ECaP with his wife. He was very ill and in the middle of a rigorous course of chemo. He was fighting a very aggressive cancer. He asked, "How did you find ECaP?"

"A therapist of mine," I replied.

He said, "I found it through Dr. Bernie Siegel. I find his work very helpful."

"I agree," I replied.

Then he looked at me with his heart shining through his eyes. I just knew a zinger was coming. He said, "You know, Michele, I have this," as he tapped a quarter-sized square spot that protruded slightly from his chest. His eyes were shining with unshed tears. "I feel for you, Michele. You wear your scar right out there all the time. I can hide mine under my shirt. I just feel so much for you, honey. Could I please give you a hug?" I was a little taken aback, but moved by the gesture. "Would that be okay?" he asked with his arms open. I nodded shyly and received a sturdy embrace. I had to give the guy credit for his boldness.

ECaP reconnected me with what inspired me, what it was that I truly yearned for in life. I liked believing in myself and in possibility. I embraced my ability to treat myself with respect and care for my body. Kevin Henry guided us through a wonderful Qi Gong workshop. We were able to gather energy and move it. Dwayne, of all people, was really impressed. It was indisputable. He actually felt the energy vibrating between his palms. That's was some really useful, motivating information. I took it with me and practiced every day.

One day, I did a cartwheel during a break in one of the sessions. There was a little bit of lawn next to the picnic area where we were working. It was a beautiful day. There had been a lot of gray days and rain recently, but this day the sun was shining. I felt inspired. Perhaps I wanted to prove something. I went out onto that lawn and I did a cartwheel. I did it to say to myself, "Yeah, you can still do a cartwheel; you can still play in the sun." I could still be myself.

ECaP was helpful for Dwayne because he got to see other partners fighting alongside their loved ones. There was a session just for the cancer supporters. They got to tell their stories and voice their pain to others who really understood. It is very difficult for the caretakers. Their journeys with cancer can be as rigorous as the patients'.

During one of the last sessions we all sat in a circle with the postcards that we had chosen to represent our hope in healing. Each would walk into the center of the circle to show his/her postcard and share. When it was Dwayne's turn to share his card, he stood and did something he rarely does— he started to cry. He held up a picture of a happy old couple riding bicycles into the sunset. He said in a broken voice, "This is how I always imagined my life with Michele. Simply growing old together, being there for each other for a very long time. I don't know how to do this thing without her." We were all moved to tears. I could not wait to hug him, my own true love.

ECaP was an awesome experience and provided me with another set of tools to Face Forward and continue to play for my life. I was now equipped to heal and put back into my life what had been missing.

The Bright Side

To be an equipped master of your life you need to have your own personal tool box. It must be stocked with everything you need to build the life you want. Managing time is a primary life task that you must instill. This is not referring to time management skills. I mean weighing the scales of your fortune firmly to the positive. You will do this day-by-day, by filling your days with creating rather than negating. You have the ability to make the future you want tomorrow, but it starts today. Make your perspective today more positive than negative. Let your story today be of what you really *want* rather than what you do not want.

Positive thoughts right before you go to bed improve tomorrow's outlook. The last thought before sleep sets the tone for the subconscious for the night. If you make the last thought before drifting off to sleep a good one it will work busily creating positively as you dream. There are some really good self-hypnosis recordings that are made to help you drift off to a pleasant sleep. This simple act of thinking positively before sleep gains you eight hours of positive vibration to start the next day. Think of the reverse: if you go to sleep on a negative note you start the day eight hours later deficient. Better to start the day with a surplus of positive.

Go Ask Buddha

A lantern shone brightly
When light was needed
And I was shown the way

After ECaP, I continued on my journey of healing. I went to the Green Mountain Dharma Center founded by Thich Nhat Hanh. Simone and I drove from her home to Vermont. We had a four-hour talk. Our conversation for over 17 years had been much the same. We talk about possibility and the power each of us holds. We discuss how we can make dreams come true. We move to express ourselves fully, so we can be revealed and understood. Simone is a well-spring of knowledge. She is well connected to the Source of her. Plants flourish in her care. Injured animals arrive at her door to be nurtured. Every moment in her presence is filled with a sense of universal awareness. Ideas and theories abounded in our chatter. Simone was able to bring clarity to some of my rusty thoughts.

It was an intense, austere weekend. There were no luxuries at the Buddhist monastery. The weather was cold and rainy. The environment was stripped to the bare basics. We used only what was needed. We took a little less than we would have liked. I had so much respect for the Buddhist sisters who opened their home to Simone and me. They lived so simply, it was beautiful and stunning to see. The sisters' heads were shaved. They wore brown robes. They honored many customs. We took off our shoes before entering a room. We stopped whatever we were doing when the bells rang, which was hourly. We meditated for hours a day. There was no light discussion. Words were used only when necessary or when it was time to speak freely. Buddhists have a deep love for all living things and are vegetarians. They do not kill or injure living things unnecessarily. It was interesting, in a wonderful way, to watch a room full of monks and sisters scurrying around trying to scoop up a spider. I did not dare move lest I accidentally step on it and kill it.

On our first morning Mother allowed us to visit with her. She had large eyes that glowed with an inner light. She did not seem of this world but rather of light and air. She spoke in a very low, quiet tone. I had to lean forward to hear her. She spoke slowly and directly, "Here we are mindful. We are conscious of our breath going in and out. Breathe in and think, 'I am calm.' Breathe out and think, 'I smile.'

"We invite you out to walk mindfully and we will meditate while we walk. We breathe in for a certain number of steps and exhale for the same amount of steps. We walk into the present moment gracefully like a lion or an elephant.

"We invite you to meditate with us. We sit very still yet we feel unbound. When we tire of our position we ask Buddha to breathe for us, to sit for us. We then breathe with loved ones of the past and present. You can breathe with your ancestors.

"We invite you to eat with us mindfully. We do not speak during meals so we can truly praise nature for our food and know how blessed we are. We eat slowly, chewing until the food is liquid in our mouths. We fully enjoy the gift of the cosmos; we taste the sunshine, the rain, the glory of earth's bounty."

I had a really intense moment during one of the longer meditation sessions. I felt like I was on a natural high. My senses were acute. I could feel all this energy buzzing around me and within me. I kind of faded into the environment and became one with everything. Then a lantern shone brightly before me. Everything looked clear and beautiful ahead. Tears of joy ran down my cheeks.

Get Absorbed

There is a warm glowing place inside of you. This is the place you seek in absorption. Perhaps you feel it when you drift off to sleep. You may feel it when you are sitting at the beach, while jogging, skiing, singing or meditating. The sources of absorption are infinite and deeply personal. That place is the best of you, your highest good. This is the power you want to align with.

A sense of good vibrations comes from connecting to that which beats your heart. Just past the ego's chatter, beyond the body's carnal desires, out of reach of the conscious mind, there you find your source. It is the stillness within, the feeling of abundance, the stirring of possibility, a remembering of sorts.

On the drive home Simone and I talked deeply. I asked her, "Simone, did you notice that I was reserved over the weekend?"

"I noticed that you were not engaging others as you normally would have done. I thought of course Michele is shy. I am sad that I did not get it. Not many probably do. You have to educate others to help them understand. It must be so tiring for you. I feel overwhelmed for you. You have had so much to process so quickly," Simone said.

As she revealed this truth I felt my defenses rise. I felt anger rear its head. I hated to feel pity directed at me. I had not asked for this change! I did not want this change! This was all so drastic and isolating. I felt so disconnected from everything I had known. Everything was different. I was different. It was not only my face that had changed, *I* had changed. Forced change was an extremely hard thing to accept.

Simple Meditation

Here's a meditation that is easy and will quickly take you into a higher vibration. Sit in a straight back chair; put your feet on the ground and your hands on your thighs. Do not cross anything so your energy may flow freely. Make the sound "Ah." Sit outside whenever you can during this practice. Let the "Ah" resound from you. Get lost in the tone you make, sense the profound release. Feel the sound fill you, making you light with its buoyancy.

Sliced For The 4Th Time

Altered, scarred
½ my smile frozen into a frown
All is not in working order
In this twisted reality
Here with myself

The infection that began in May stayed with me until December. It was cut out in a fourth operation just before Christmas. Nothing was closing the hole. Then another fissure popped open. I now had two pencil-width sized holes oozing green puss from the side of my head. By the time November came around, one side of my head was the size of two heads. There was constant pain and a hot burning sensation. The IV antibiotics did not stop it. Time wasn't healing these wounds.

"Michele, we're going to have to remove the entire fat graft," Dr. Costantino told me.

My mind was whirling. "What does that mean?" I asked, not really wanting to know. I knew the fat graft had been placed there to make my face more symmetrical after the parotid gland was removed. Now they had to remove that balance, my face would look concave on one side.

In preparation for my fourth operation, I asked to be given Valium beforehand to make things easier for me. I stayed pretty calm, but I had become much less tolerant about entering the operating room. Something had begun to break down in me and I would just cry. I was so overwhelmed by fear. I just wanted it to be over quickly.

In this fourth operation they removed so much of the side of my face there was now a red, raw hole about the size of a fist where my ear should have been. I was now even more imperfect, grotesque even, and open to the world. I had to push several feet of gauze into the hole twice a day and then remove it. I was like this insane magician pulling scarves out of my face. Instead it was gauze, oozing green with smelly puss and blood.

After this latest setback, I decided to go away to Jamaica with Dwayne, Nicole and her husband, Jesse. I was going to look at the beautiful Caribbean Sea. I would feel the Trade Winds blow on my face and feel alive, even though I was walking around with a fleshy gaping hole in my head that I could not get wet. I still went into the sea on a paddle boat. I also spent my time on a raft or wading in up to my waist. The sea was meant for me. I remember Nikki and I screaming laughing as we paddled back to shore like a mad woman because we saw a stingray. That was very funny, a tickled pink moment. *Yeah, I was doing my thing.*

New Year's Eve night was very challenging for me. Things were not the same. I did not look or feel the same. It was hard dealing with the whole Happy New Year thing; all that hugging and kissing. I just had to leave. I said my Happy New Years as politely as I could. Then I spent some time with my husband. We both got on the better side of tipsy and made love in the Jacuzzi. I was just glad to have him with me on this crazy journey.

I was aware of how difficult this was for Dwayne. His beautiful wife was taken from him and he was left with a changed woman, a woman who certainly looked different. He is the first to remind me that I am 99% the same, only one tiny percent of me has changed. I love the way he looks at life. I would say, "Dwayne, you are my very staunchest supporter. I love you so very much."

Once I returned from Jamaica, all I wanted to do was strap on my skis and hit the slopes. I needed the sense of freedom skiing gave me. I had to have my ski-pass photo taken. I did not like pictures of me and asked people not to take them. Pictures were undeniable proof of the cold hard facts. I had the picture taken but I dared not look at it immediately. As soon as I saw my photograph, I cried. My paralyzed face stared back at me. It was stark. It was a blatant reminder that I wore my imperfection for the world to see.

As difficult as it was to see that photo, it was worth it because there is nothing like skiing for me. I loved the sound of the snow beneath my skis, the feel of the wind against my body as I glided through winter's stillness. Strapping those skis on gave me a sense of total freedom. It was a beautiful thing. I lived for skiing. I loved the 20-minute drive down the long winding country roads surrounded by farms, old red barns, woodlands, mountains and lakes. I would scream out my pain and agony in song. I cried and sobbed in despair and disbelief. However, as soon as my skis hit the slopes I felt at one with everything. I understood what it meant to be blessed; I was marvelously alive.

Busted

Driving
Moving through the scenery
Momentum
Keeping alive the dream of me
My face, a sign post
Makes another
Stop and look again
Challenging
The social norms book

Unfortunately, I broke my knee about six weeks into my new-found freedom. My right eye is tricky and will not withstand the use of contacts. I cannot ski with glasses because they get fogged up. So I wore no glasses. I did not see the difference in texture between two adjoining slopes. As I skied over the groomed corduroy slope the tip of one ski got caught in the ice. I kept moving. My knee did a 180-degree turn. I knew it was bad because I could not get up. It was almost as if I had no knee at all and my legs were made of water. I was embarrassed when the ski patrol had to ski me down the mountain on a stretcher. It was the kind of thing that I used to gape at from the chair lift thinking, *Some poor bastard just got hurt bad.*

I needed radical knee surgery. I had broken my knee in three different places: my meniscus, my ACL and MCL. I had really messed it up. I could not believe that I was out of commission again! I was not able to walk or care for my daughter. Poor Dwayne looked so frustrated and volatile. Thankfully, Dwayne's parents, Hazel and Aundrea, and my mother were there to lend us helping hands. I don't know how we would have made it without their help.

I had been through four surgeries in nine months and now I would need a fifth operation, on my knee. This was the most physically painful surgery of all because after the anesthesia wore off I was in extreme pain. The first five days they wanted me to bend my knee regularly. It was agony. I could barely stand or walk. I cried to my mother the day after the operation, the pain was so unbearable. "Mom, I think I've hit the threshold of endurance. I cannot take any more pain." My mom just let me cry it out. "I know Michie," she replied. I knew she wanted to take my pain away.

Shortly after surgery, I had to go to my accountant's office, which was on the second floor of his building. Dwayne had to park two blocks away, so I had to crutch my way through the crowded streets of Manhattan's fashion district. My face was all swollen, red, raw and lopsided. My hair was half shaven off. My face was full of acne, and my knee was broken. I was crutching down the street, my half head of hair flying everywhere. I had stupidly forgotten a hat. I made it up the stairs sweating and windblown, looking like a crazy woman. The accountant saw me, gave a nervous laugh and said, "You know, Michele, I just feel so bad for you." His partner at the next desk did a double take. My accountant said, "This is Michele, she used to be an investment banker. Her face is twisted because she had cancer." His words felt like a slap in the face, a very cold reality.

We were feeling the financial sting of my expensive health care. We felt strain, fear and uncertainty. I considered returning to work. I even went so far as to line up a job at my old firm. Following my knee surgery, there was no way I was going back to the world of investment banking with a twisted, lopsided face, hobbling on a broken knee. My soul was stating in clear terms that I was not to go back there. I took this as a sign. I was to keep still. This break stopped me from moving in the direction that I would have returned to instinctively. I was heading in a new direction. It became clear that this series of traumatic experiences was to help me recognize the need to change directions. The knee surgery simply sealed the deal.

Through all of the pain I could see that I was rediscovering the woman I had not been in years. I was becoming a woman of strength, of glory, of wisdom, of grace, all the things I had promised myself in college that I would become. I did not like my circumstances one bit. I did like who they had forced me to rediscover. There was a lot of work to be done yet. I had to shed the peripheral distractions that had each taken a piece of my spirit. I needed to become whole. I was learning what my universal truths were. The lessons that came my way were sweet. They revived my spirit.

Wounds Explained

I wake up some days so angry
Searching in the mirror for yesterday
Am I still there?
Good days and bad
I try for more good
I am frightened
There are so many firsts
And I'm already in the middle

My three siblings and their children came to visit. In total there were eight additional people in the house. I thought I handled it well, but I had my moments. Playing hostess was always a bit of a pain for me, even with the most helpful of guests. I was excited for people to comment on the improvement with my smile. My sister, Nicole, commented several times. My older sister Sydney and my brother Brad did not say a thing. Finally, on Sunday outside in the snow, I approached my brother and asked, "Do you want to see the improvement?"

I smiled, my upper lip lifting ever so slightly. He squinted like he did not see any difference. Mind you it was not a full balanced smile but you could now see teeth on the right side when there were no teeth to be seen just three months before. I could see I would have to explain the changes to him. "Do you remember this did not move at all?" I said pointing to my lip, one of the branches of my facial nerve had regenerated. *Amazing, a miracle?* Brad responded, "Well you look great to me. I mean, to you it must still be a big thing. To me, you only notice it for the first two minutes and then you don't notice it at all."

This highlighted a phenomenon I began to recognize—people who love me didn't really seem able to deal with the reality I faced. They seemed to have a hard time digesting the fact that my every interaction with people was affected—that some people stared agog and then turned away disgusted. To the rest of the world I was abnormal. I was no longer part of the norm. My friends and family did not understand that this happens all the time. It was too hard for them to acknowledge.

I felt the tears welling up in my eyes as I realized I would have to expose myself to help him understand the reality that I faced. I said, "Brad, we have to first accept that I am now disfigured." He looked incredulous, shaking his head and I just nodded mine. I explained, "Please understand that America is a visual society. In those first two minutes that seem like nothing to you, I am weighed, measured and many times dismissed." I tried to explain further, "It doesn't make me sad all the time, Brad, but this reality has certainly impacted my life. It will always impact my life. The fact is that I am changed."

It still nicked me emotionally when people stared or looked uncomfortable. When I mentioned it to Dwayne with tears in my eyes, he playfully smacked me in the face and said, "You're alive," as he hugged me tight. I dealt with it as best I could. Over time I learned to just let people's reactions pass over me.

I had to continually remind myself that it was not about the end result but the process. I was actively involved in getting on with my life, the sweet stuff of living. I had a loving husband who wanted me to live and supported me. Dwayne and I had weathered many storms. I knew he was my rock. I could count on him as we continued to move in overcast seas with unpredictable turnings of the tide.

Take a Load Off

Take a huge load off your shoulders. Look at where you can forgive in your life. Holding on to anger and past hurt only hurts you. It blocks your vital energy from flowing freely. A practice of forgiveness that is very easy and wonderfully rewarding is just four simple phrases. Say them in any order you prefer: 'I love you, I am sorry, please forgive me, thank you.' I understand this is called Ho'oponopono and is an ancient Hawaiian practice that clears old programming, helps you forgive, and plain makes you feel better. You can use this peaceful practice in any number of ways. Say the phrases over and over, in song, whispered under your breath, silently in your head, or aloud as is a prayer. You can offer it to yourself or dedicate it to someone you love or a cause you feel strongly about. Good on you.

The Real Deal

Living Into My Life
There is this lump of clay
My life
I am actively molding it
Shaping its form
I am getting somewhere
Just the other day someone commented on it
"Ah, yes... I see it now...yes
It's a woman in joy"

Dwayne chuckled and shook his head as he glanced over at me. We shared a moment, both not quite believing where life had taken us. Here we were in the endless mountains of Pennsylvania, living in a lovely three bedroom A-frame, on seven country acres with a small pond, surrounded by dairy farms. There was even a time when there were 50 head of bison just up the road. It had been a long day, but happily at the end of it Dwayne had a wad of cash in his pocket from food sales. We had our own hot food truck industrial lunch route. He was driving the truck the 60 miles home. As our truck rattled down the country roads, my mind started to wander, meandering through my life. I could always be counted on to be the pioneer with the heart of an adventurer.

Even years before cancer I felt a driving need to change perspective. After September 11th and then my father's passing I told Dwayne, "We have to have something away from the city, something to clean the soot and dirt from our nostrils, a chance to breathe fresh air. I cannot keep working for just a good time. I need a change of perspective. Let's go and buy a house close to Tracy and Craig's ski house." Tracy has been a bosom friend since I was 16 but when my father was dying she showed her true colors and was my steadfast refuge. Many a night Dwayne and I would run to Tracy and Craig's for respite in their idyllic suburban back yard and their warm company.

We had spent a lovely week with Tracy and Craig and their kids in PA skiing. We knew we wanted a country home one day. Dwayne agreed. He began to scour the Internet for opportunities within ten miles from the ski mountain. Dwayne had always wanted land, so the search had to have at least five acres. When Dwayne found the place we finally bought, we drove in the deep dark winter to the house. There must have been nine feet of snow on the ground, but we fell in love. I sighed at the thought of our quiet country home and field stone wall lined drive. Thank goodness for it or where would I have gone to nurture and heal myself?

Despite needing to heal from the fissures leaking foul smelling fluid from my head, having my face literally pulled away from my skull, or undergoing radiation that seared me to the bone, I still read. I took notes. I attended lectures. I even joined Real Estate Investment clubs. I would drive 70 miles each way to a meeting with other real estate investors in the dark of the night on those long lonely country roads. Despite my misshapen head and my reservation in my appearance, I just went for it.

I knew that I had to find a passive income stream to help make way for a future. Real estate was a tangible vehicle that really interested me. I set myself on a course of study that would have earned me a graduate degree if they were given for home study. For endless hours before making my first investment property purchase, I strategized and set up due diligence processes. I built quite an extensive real estate investment library at home.

I was so proud of myself and Dwayne for the life we carved out for ourselves. We are entrepreneurs who are willing to do what it takes. Our hot truck business had had quite the history, from when Dwayne catered for the film industry in New York City, or sold his fare at Home Depot in Brooklyn, or on the streets of Manhattan. In Pennsylvania we built a hot food lunch route serving prefabricated home builders and truckers in an industrial park outside Scranton. We hit every parade, country fair and festival possible.

I was an entrepreneur from the first. When I was in seventh grade there was a discount store that sold every kind of candy, four for one dollar. I would bike two miles each way every day to buy my inventory for the next day. At school I would sell my fair wares for $.50 and double my money. So every day I would buy more candy to make more money. I did that until the store went out of business just a month later.

When I was in grad school, I invested in a multi-tiered business where they were selling 900 numbers, discount coupons, and satellite dishes. We had a total of twelve business lines all selling different services. Every weekend, we would canvass a different neighborhood leaving flyers on every car.

On the food route we served prefabricated home builders. We met a lot of craftsmen, including carpenters, roofers, electricians, plumbers, and painters. Dwayne was the order and money taker. I was the short-order, fry cook. It was a hive of activity but there were many conversations held while waiting for an order. From all of my studies it was apparent we were in an ideal area to invest in properties that we could leverage to earn passive income. Ever since the illness I knew I was an unlikely candidate for life insurance. I became very focused on passive income that could serve as an annuity for my family.

Real estate investments have been the foundation of many families' wealth. My chosen strategy was to buy low and hold long term. I began to look at the local paper for properties for sale in a small city along the truck route. I happened on a property listed significantly under market. I drove by the house; it was a lovely old Victorian a little down at the heels. Neglect was apparent but I could only see opportunity. I hurried home to tell Dwayne about it. I was speaking quickly as I often do when I'm excited about something. I described the opportunity. I had studied over 50 books on real estate. I had recently gone to a real estate investing seminar. I knew this was the real deal.

I had come back invigorated and determined to begin investing. Dwayne knew it was coming and here it was. We were going deep into new waters. We had better learn to swim fast. We had always been buoyant. We would stay afloat, somehow, some way… for sure.

I had created many templates on inspecting real estate and analyzing the return on investment for potential property purchases. This house looked to be an ideal first investment. I negotiated the priced down even further just before the closing.

We cut out our teeth on this first rental property. We really dove into deep rehab and landlord waters, taking on that old property with derelict tenants. We faced every problem imaginable: updating electricity, running new plumbing, refurbishing boilers, laying floors, rebuilding porches, siding a many cornered structure, roofing a multi-tiered roof, new windows, new flooring, new kitchens and bath. Everything was touched in that house. We got taken by contractors we had to sue. It was quite the adventure. On the other side sat a lovely restored Victorian side by side double. Two families could live there and raise their children. I know that Dwayne really enjoys the feeling of going to the P.O. box and picking up rents. I must admit I do too. It is quite satisfying to earn money while I sleep. That property led us to many more. Real estate now is the cornerstone of our business. I never cease to feel a deep abiding sense of comfort that this income will continue long into the future. ***So there, insurance companies***! I have insured myself and my family with an annuity in the form of long term rents.

You Got This

Concentration becomes key to your success. To concentrate is to focus your mind on a given desire until ways and means for its realization have been worked out successfully by your subconscious and put into operation. Suggestion and habit are two of the most important influences on concentration. A habit is a mental path over which your actions have traveled for some time. Each pass makes the path a little deeper and a bit wider. This mental rut becomes the path of least resistance.

Failure is only momentary defeat. It should be viewed as a blessing in disguise. Your current course is halted. You are forced to redirect your efforts along more advantageous pathways. Mistakes are made so you can learn and profit from them. Sound character is built upon overcoming set backs. Every defeat teaches a needed lesson if you are willing to learn it. Realize that disuse brings only atrophy and decay. Strength and growth come only through continuous effort and struggle. You can attain stupendous heights depending on how you interpret your past experiences. Use those experiences as the basis of future working plans. Failure is just nature's way of helping prepare you for your greatness.

It is through the medium of thought that you become captain of your journey. The fact is that you are the maker of your own lot in life. Your thoughts and actions are the tools you use. Every thought you release changes your character in exact accord with it. You are punishing yourself with every wrong you commit. You reward yourself with every constructive act. Your positive thoughts develop your dynamic personality. Try to be tolerant with yourself and others. Live and let live. Interact with others as positively as possible every time. You reap what you sow. Know that the results of every thought you think are returned to you.

Turning The Page

The world
Your art gallery
Life
Your painting
You have the power to paint your
Life, day, hour, minute, second
Any color you want to
What a terrible gift to waste
So Paint. Damn it.
PLEASE PAINT!

Sometimes in life, we get the chance to close the book on the past. At a time when life presented me with a take it or leave it choice, I chose to take it. After all, doing nothing sounds just like what it is: nothing. In those decisive moments, which for me were usually accompanied by a big change or loss, I looked to the possibilities. I chose not to burn with the agonies of uncertainty and fear. When the bridge to my past was gone, there was no other choice but to move forward without looking back. I began to make incredible progress on my life's journey.

It was a gift to be able to step back and meet myself on the road, even in that harsh light. I was who I was because of what I had habituated myself to be. Life brought me to a precipice and asked me to trust and jump or stay stuck and die. I could not stay stuck. There was no longer the safe familiarity of what I had known. I jumped, propelled by necessity. I let myself fall. I realized that the distance was not nearly as great as I had feared. I nurtured my belief in myself. I trusted myself wholly for the first time in my life.

You are Safe

To get where you want to go, you need to believe you will be safe when you get there. This is not a conscious thing. Most beliefs are programs instilled in those first early years of your life when you were passively absorbing everything around you. Do you time and again almost attain a goal, and then sabotage yourself at the finish line? If so, then you know that there is a subconscious fear that the result would not be a safe place for you. Take safety into your experience. Actively tell yourself you are safe. When you think of your goal, let yourself know it is safe and all will be well. So be it, so it is.

By listening to my higher self I had found the amazing power to ask better questions. I had a problem-solving mind always seeking answers to the questions I posed. The tricky thing about my wonderful mind before cancer was that it created problems just to be able to solve them. I did not use it constructively. This mind, led by my ego, made me think that it defined me. It had weighed and measured me, and found me wanting. I discarded this useless wandering mind. I started directing the show. Source of me, an infinite wellspring, supported and guided me.

Leading Questions

You have this amazing power to ask better questions. Every thought begins with a question. You have a problem-solving-mind. It will endeavor to solve any problem you throw its way. You can center your questions around health, or whatever you most desire: love, kindness, abundance, joy, strength, or relationship.

You can ask these questions in the shower. Ask in rounds of three for each question. Start each round of questions with:

How can I...?
What will I do that...?
Wouldn't it be great if...?

A well-known saying goes: "A brave man dies once and a coward dies 1000 deaths." Could all my uneasiness and fear be settled down by a little silence? Absolutely, for within the walls of silence laid my inner voice, my true self. This was not my ego. It was the essence of me and the blessed Source of my life. I have my part to play in the never-ending story. Every great effort and effect is begun from the silence within.

For me cancer wiped the slate clean of all false pretenses. I walked exposed. It was my challenge to rise to. It was okay if those around me were not equipped for the journey because I was enough. I fell in love with myself. I rediscovered my joy. I became a cancer thriver, who grows through anything. I made hard sacrifices that gave me another day. I was there. I was scared but present and accounted for. I emerged a better, stronger me. I was a bad-ass warrior woman. I faced forward. I started in the direction I was intended to go.

My Truth Apparent

The optimist
I cannot help if I am an optimist
I cannot not care because caring is scarce
If this is a sin; I do not seek penance
If this is wrong; I beg no forgiveness
For I know it is a painful way I follow
Scarred I am and will become
But not so that I become Callous
So Scarred that I cannot feel -
I leave my heart an open shutter that pain and
Joy come flooding through.
For this is the way that I walk and
This is the path that I follow
I feel it is a lonely time ahead
But ...
My hand is always open
If you want to come walk with me

Eventually, I became this phenomenal woman who was just herself. I learned not to take on energy that did not belong to me. In other words, I did not worry about what any one else thought. I knew I was enough. I was here and I was strong. I was still tearful at times. *It was not easy.* I became more present than ever. I felt empowered to be me. I enjoyed a crisper sense of myself. I liked myself. I wanted to get to know myself better. I was worth it.

I had so many pictures of myself through the years, always smiling. This is now, that was then. I thought of myself as beautiful. Then I met beauty in another form. I became closer to myself, my spirit. My inner beauty was the Source of me.

When I held my daughter Sage in my arms, I felt blessed with abundance. Love blossomed. I experienced bliss. It was easy to stay in the moment with her. The sadness happened when I lived in my head. It was so easy to wander down the path of regrets and ask the unanswerable why. I felt the pull of my old habitual doubts that I was not good enough. I would not succumb to my ego's power play cloaked in self-criticism. I turned toward the truth and knew that I was enough.

I became the witness. I created a space outside myself where I could watch my personality's actions without judgment. The truth was that my body was constantly remaking itself. If I could control my focus and not let stress rule my reactions, I could change the patterns of illness. I focused on my natural right to vibrant health. I acted as if I was already healed, already whole. I was my source, therefore I was perfect. I discovered Divinity is being, not doing.

I had the ability to go through my body and ask each organ and tissue to be restored to perfect health. I filled my body with golden light and saw every cell restored. I visualized a comb removing toxins and debris.

I had to know what I really desired so I could make the ends justify the means. What inspired me? What was my life's dream? It was time to re-evaluate what mattered most. It was really an incredible growth opportunity. I needed to design a survival program that I could stick with. I had to stay inspired and be passionate. Everyday I needed to wake up and Face Forward.

I needed to find calm in the midst of chaos. I explored activities that helped me and brought me peace. I engaged in them regularly.

Burning Desire

You can acquire everything you need to attain your main ideal by organizing all your knowledge. Develop that knowledge into power. This creates a bridge over all your weaknesses. To be successful in living life, you are required to be able to change the color of your mind. You will resemble, tomorrow, the dominating thoughts of your mind today. Plant a seed for tomorrow wisely. Frame your life in your mind's eye. Seek out and speak of the good.

Your mind develops and grows through use. Nature hates a void and in her dominion idleness leads to waste. Mental inertia is so common. A stagnant mind is the breeding place of fear. Your most treacherous adversary is fear. Your main underlying fear is the fear of death. Fear has six basic forms: fear of lack, fear of demise, fear of failing health, fear of the loss of affection, fear of growing old, and fear of disapproval. Your fears must be mastered before you can reach your highest potential. Fear will not just disappear. You must push through it.

The struggle to eke out a stable existence in these harried materialistic times is immense. Many find it easier to drift aimlessly through life. To succeed, it is of critical importance to learn to organize and direct your natural talents toward a specific intention. Harness the power of your mind by stimulating it with strong desire. Your mind, once stimulated by a strong desire, can become a harnessed power. Your actions will always reflect your predominant frame of mind. Singleness of purpose is vital for success. You are now engaged in training for success.

Using a system of allowing can help you move through life with minimum resistance and friction. Success is the power to manifest what you intend in life. Power is the organized effort that builds the foundation of abundance from the convergence of facts, knowledge and capabilities. When you live in your power you radiate confidence. You understand and apply organized effort in the attainment of your goals.

I weeded out all the negative thoughts. I planted positive ones in their place. I was excited about my personal power. The fact that my thoughts affect my body gave me the power to create. I took deep cleansing breaths and brought myself back to the stillness of the present. I detached myself from the odds and embraced my wellness. I asked myself, *Whoever said I was average?* I believed I would age like fine wine. I planned on getting better and better.

I fought to re-imagine myself each day. I liked to believe that I would live a long life with Dwayne. There is an old Indian saying, "If you want to know what your thoughts were yesterday, look at your life today. If you want to know what your future will be, look to your thoughts today." With the old me, questions and worries just bogged down my soul. I understood whatever I focused on would manifest itself in the future. I spent much time working with my breath.

An Introduction to Transformational Breath

I am Tanya Rothstein, a co-trainer with the Transformational Breath Foundation. I had the honor of facilitating a number of sessions with Michele. Transformational Breath is a self-empowering, deeply healing process co-created by Dr. Judith Kravitz that has brought great transformation into Michele's life. This dynamically powerful technique utilizes a high vibrational energy source created by a specific breathing pattern. Michele reported better breathing, more physical energy, better health, as well as resolution of stress and mental and emotional issues.

The life-altering motion of Transformational Breathing created an entrainment effect at the cellular level of Michele's electromagnetic field. The universal law of entrainment states that when two things come together that are operating at different rates, the lower vibration will automatically be raised to match the higher vibration. By breathing larger quantities of high vibrational oxygen into previously closed parts of Michele's respiratory system, Michele's dense lower vibratory patterns

Continued on next page…

...continued from previous page

such as old emotions, traumas and dis-ease were brought to a higher frequency and permanently resolved. Michele felt lighter and clearer after being bathed with this higher vibrational energy.

The first level of Michele's healing journey in Transformational Breath included restructuring her breathing. Michele's air volume increased significantly. This, in turn, played a significant role in treating and eliminating disease.

By improving her breathing capacity, Michele had more energy to experience life, better health, more balance, increased detoxification, improved respiratory capacity, and a stronger immune system. Transformational Breathing teaches that the amount of air that we bring into the body is directly related to the amount of good we can accept in life. Michele found to the degree that the breath is open and flowing she is in the flow of life.

The second level of healing in these breathing sessions allowed Michele to access her subconscious realm where her mental and emotional traumas are stored. These traumas played a major role in shutting down Michele's breathing. These traumas, stored at the cellular level, are also called old unexpressed emotions, (repressions), negative beliefs, deep hurts, resentments, old tapes and past memories. One of the primary ways that Michele kept things "stuffed" in the subconscious was to shut down and control her breathing. Through facilitation Michele was able to breathe into the closed places and "let go" where she had previously held onto her breath. As old emotions, thoughts, and memories surfaced, she continued to breathe into them, thus easily integrating them into a higher energy form. During her breath sessions, Michele was able to resolve traumas resulting from getting cancer, having surgery, and undergoing other recovery processes. Once these major areas of dysfunction were resolved, limiting and self-sabotaging behavior dropped away. Her true and perfect self more fully emerged.

Continued on next page...

...continued from previous page

Michele's clearing of her lower subconscious created an opening to the higher subconscious which is the level of the soul and spiritual awareness. This third level of Transformational Breath allowed Michele to come in contact more fully with her higher aspects of self. Her spiritual healing journey has resulted in Michele's producing even more love, joy, and well-being in her life and activating her powerful contracts and missions for this lifetime.

I looked at my healing in a holistic light. I treated my whole person, my mind, body and spirit. I integrated Eastern and Western medicine. My brain was geared for questions, so I asked myself better questions. My brain was programmed to find the answers so I leveraged this amazing power. My good questions began with: How can I...? What can I do...? I did not ask "Why...?" It would only cause struggle. I felt tough and gritty. I would rise to this ocassion. Every step of the way I was there, re-creating my life, through the focus of my thoughts.

I developed self trust and followed my spirit as it manifested itself through me. I listened to the higher wisdom of my heart. I worked through issues of betrayal and mistrust. I fought the tendency to trust everyone but myself. I trusted myself and accessed higher principles to guide me to integrity. I let my mind surrender to the wisdom of the heart. I remembered that the spirit shines through me. I forgave myself my mistakes.

I put faith in myself. I asked for guidance. I was honest with my feelings. I stayed flexible in all situations. I became authentic in my "Yes" or "No."

I geared all of my time, energy and focus on banishing cancer. I knew I had to love myself today, even if I might not be here tomorrow. I allowed myself to be a mess if that was how I felt. I tried to be as I was. I did not struggle to put a good face on things.

I got depressed but I knew that I had the power to decide. I could focus my thoughts and send better messages to my body. Whatever happened I could handle it. I learned to trust that everything I needed would be there when I needed it. My mind was a powerful healer. I could visualize healing occurring within me, anytime. I was in charge. I knew what was best for me. I became responsible for my needs.

The year following my diagnosis was filled with infection and a total of five operations. During that period some doors closed and others opened. That first year all I could do was concentrate on healing the infection and winning my wellness back. I felt that I had been chewed up and spit out; just a mockery of my former self. Irreparably damaged, I considered that vat of pain pills standing ready to help me numb out and withdraw.

However, I was a natural born optimist. I was particularly rebellious in my youth and early adulthood. There was no taking away the woman I had spent 32 years becoming. My emergency forces were invigorated and they charged to my rescue. I gathered all the resources I could. They came in various forms—loved ones, gifts, books, Emotional Freedom Tapping, SPOHNC, Bloch Foundation, Live Strong, and positive practices and philosophy – blessings delivered as if they had been pre-ordered.

I had nothing but time to dedicate to processing and healing. I was there in the moment, not in my waning past of ease and comfort. I now stood on the outside looking in at normalcy. For so long I had considered myself lucky, never really believing how easy it had been for me. Then I became what I had believed: flawed, not good enough.

If I wanted to see my past thoughts, all I had to do was to look at myself in the present. If I wanted a future, I had to control my thoughts one moment at a time. It is incredibly difficult to be stared at by people, sometimes open mouthed, whispering behind cupped hands, nudging each other to ensure no one misses me. It is a very difficult thing to hear parents explain to children the reason for my twisted face or discipline them for innocently mimicking it. I worried once and asked Dwayne, "What will we say when Sage asks why mommy looks different?" He hugged me and said, "We will tell her that Mommy sacrificed her smile to be with you today." I nodded, tears of love burned my eyes.

Speak It

Words hold so much power. Words can cause a positive or negative effect. Powerless words should be deleted from your vocabulary. Some of the words you use so frequently can be hindrances in disguise. If you say, "I am trying to be better" you are giving yourself an out. *Trying* never gets you there; it is a word that leaves you in the middle of the road. *Trying* gives you an inherent excuse to be ineffective.

If you are always *hoping* for something, then you are hedging your bets. *Hoping* is a word that leaves a shadow of doubt. You can also *want* something a lot, but when you *want*, you are coming from a place of scarcity. To *want* has an energy of lack which has a tendency to pull insufficiency toward you.

Make the commitment to yourself to remove these disempowering words from your vocabulary. One simple way to say all these words in a positive way is not to try, or hope, or want, but to *intend* and to *be*. So start saying, "I *intend that…*" or "*I am…*" Own your speech and frame it in this positive way. You can change the direction of this moment and the next, and subsequently improve your whole life.

You've Come A Long Way Baby

I go
Still
I go

My tragic journey has led me to transform my life. I gently planted small, positive seedlings in my focus. Over time I have honored and nurtured my focus, positively training it daily. I have grown strong like an oak, though sometimes I can bend like a willow. I am healthy and well, empowered and strong. I am a fierce, fiery version of myself. I am nothing less than a Phoenix, reborn in flame and fury.

Life is pain and pleasure wrapped up like a bittersweet fruit. The art of life comes into play when your life is one hot mess. When my life was a gore fest I stopped fighting and let myself allow. I began to practice how I would like to be. My intentional affirmations are posted on my mirror. I intend them every day as I do my hair. I wear and use color to express my truth. In the shower I sing the Prayer of Jabez, through that prayer I ask to be taken out of my comfort zone, to always feel safe and to only do good unto others. Then I ask myself rounds of leading questions on how to live my highest and best life. I sing all the time, every day, whenever I can. I hold words sacred and in song I honor them.

Color Your Life

Colors are everywhere, just take a look around. Mother Nature presents you with an array of the rainbow everyday, from the pink of the sunrise to the green of the grass. When you wear colors you speak to and express your power. Each color has the potential to bring something different to your day. It becomes a pleasure to dress in the morning as you choose what you will say to yourself and others through your expression of color.

I decided to trust, to just plain have faith. It works for me. I have conviction that all will be well, even when life feels like a living hell. This serves me, too. Magic started happening in my life on a regular basis. I was able to believe in something and see it come to me by sheer force of will and focus.

Some really amazing things have happened for me on this journey. As my path became my goal, I learned to love life's uncertainties because I am certain of me. Whenever I needed, I was given. Resources abounded Annette introduced me to mantras, Marie O'Neil assisted me in consistently connecting to Source, Jennie Falco guided me to highest good. Susana helped open doors to vital connections. Roxanne Hulderman united me with my personal angels.

I just had to reach for the essence of what I needed in my mind and I called it to me. Dear friends, like Jessica, Jenny, Eileen, and Simone Dugger travelled great distances to be there present with me. Andrea would be a sounding board that I could rely on for constructive feedback. Through a consistency of focus, I have given my attention to that which has helped my smile grow. I began to Receive and Believe all that would help me live my highest and best life.

My marriage is a testament to two people actively working it out. We each stake our claim yet yield alternately in a gracious give and take. My mother said at my wedding, "Marriage is like a see-saw, when one is up many times the other is down. The goal is to keep the see-saw moving and enjoy those glorious moments of balance."

Our lovely Sage is now older sister to her brother, Malachi. The news of Malachi was a bit of a drama. The day I missed my period I knew immediately. I felt it in my gut; *I was pregnant*. I was on my way from NY to DC to visit Nikki with our dearest friend, Dawn. When we arrived I did not even let us get comfortable. I made everyone run to the drugstore to get an early pregnancy test. Nikki and I stood in her bathroom staring at the test stick, watching the plus sign growing clearer. It was confirmed, I was pregnant. This was a major deal.

I was overjoyed though I knew Dwayne was going to freak out. The most important thing to him is that I live on. I knew he was going to worry. The doctors told me not to have a second child. The risk of pregnancy increased the risk of the return of any latent cancer. I was so devastated by the news, not to have another child that I nearly collapsed into a puddle of tears on a New York City sidewalk. Now six years into health, I was holding another life in my hands. For me there was no question. It was a fact that I was having a child. There was no other decision possible.

Those who loved me could feel my fiery determination but they were afraid for my life. The first voice of concern was Nikki's because she was right there. She knew a decision had to be made quickly. She wanted to make sure I was aware and took into account all of the factors. She made sure it was clear that all those who loved me put my health first. Then there was Dwayne who just loves me and wants me to live a long life. He is also a natural born father. Honestly he is probably one of the greatest fathers I've ever seen. He loves children. He is like the pied piper to them. But for him, I always come first in his mind.

On the ride home Dawn and I talked soulfully, as we have done many times throughout our lives. I told her about how there was no choice for me, in all honesty my arms ached to hold my baby. We had wanted a baby so badly that we were planning to go to India that January to arrange for a surrogate to carry our child. We were both fertile. A child born through surrogacy would have been fine. The child would be from us but not born of me. Well, life threw us a curveball. Now the child would be born of me. Dawn, as she always does, listened attentively with love and caring. By the time I returned home I felt cleansed and sure. We were welcoming a new baby into this world.

The pregnancy went well and for most of it I was told that the baby was a girl. In my very fiber I knew that the child was a boy no matter what anyone said. There was no way to convince me any differently. Dwayne talked himself blue trying to get me to accept that the baby was a girl. I would just reply, "Dwayne just be ready to run after your son, Malachi." We planned to name him after my maternal grandfather, a successful entrepreneur and real estate investor from Trinidad.

I finally had agreed with Dwayne that if the seven month scan showed the baby was a girl, I would accept it. I would welcome our daughter Grace to the world. So when the tech said "it's a girl" during that scan I was just thinking, *Welcome sweet baby girl Grace, we love you.* Then I heard a squeak of surprise from the tech "Oh, oh, oh, we have a boy here!" Again I was reminded to trust my intuition. Malachi arrived with his eyes open, voracious for life. We welcomed him with profound joy. Malachi's birth gave reason to everything that came before him.

I take on new adventures. I am quite the biking enthusiast. An acquaintance said the other day "Wow, you are quite the weekend warrior." That made me smile. Dawn (my riding impetus) and I ride the NYC 5 Boro Ride with about 25,000 other riders. Through rain or shine, every year we ride. Dawn gave me a plaque that says it all so well: *She believed she could so she did.*

Dwayne and I have grown quite a real estate property portfolio, most of them we own free and clear. Dwayne has found his second profession. He is a great property manager. Our tenants stay and stay. We are responsive and reliable landlords. We actually care about our properties and our tenants. We take an eye sore and restore a neighborhood. We are proud to provide quality housing. Many times it's the best housing our tenants have experienced. We do this profitably and generate solid passive income. We have created a successful and workable real estate investing system that really works for us.

We go back and forth from the country to the city, especially during ski season. Sage is a little skiing ace. The view from my condo is of the West Side NYC skyline from the George Washington Bridge to the Verrazano Bridge. It is breathtaking and inspiring. It is so nice to have a completely different environment to go to. It helps keep things in perspective. I am always cleansed and at ease when returning to nature in beautiful Pennslyvania. I am rejuvenated and energized by the city. I love the mix. I feel blessed to live this contrast.

I know all is possible. We see fireworks on a regular basis just out of the blue over the Hudson outside our 45th floor window. We feel blessed and celebrated. We know, deeply and profoundly what we have. Sometimes Dwayne and I gaze over the heads of our children at each other and the love just flows.

My paralyzed face has been miraculous. From the first it did what it was not supposed to be able to do. My eye blinked when they said it was not supposed to. There were no nerves left controlling the closure. Nonetheless I blink and have for many years. On top of that little miracle, one of my five facial nerves regenerated. Can you believe it? It grew back from nothing. Although diagnosed to be paralyzed forever, my face now moves. In my unique lopsided way, I grin, even smile.

Life and nature with its tenacious spirit will always surprise you. Please let it delight you with its cleverness. Allow the wonder in.

Part II

Your power starts from the point you decide to take your control back.

21 Insights to Thriving

The 3 Principles of Prosperity

Through the Principle of Perception you will

Insight 1: Wake Up

I prefer to be true to myself, even at the hazard of incurring the ridicule of others, rather than to be false, and to incur my own abhorrence.
Frederick Douglass

Insight 2: Control the Power of Your Story

It's not the events of our lives that shape us, but our beliefs as to what those events mean.
Tony Robbins

Insight 3: Get Aligned

Our thinking and our behavior are always in anticipation of a response. It is therefore fear-based.
Deepak Chopra

Insight 4: Use Fabulous Energy

The roots of all goodness lie in the soil of appreciation for goodness.
Dalai Lama

Insight 5: Sublimely Self Suggest

To discover what you really believe, pay attention to the way you act— and to what you do when things don't go the way you think they should. Pay attention to what you value. Pay attention to how and on what you spend your time.
Geneen Roth

Insight 6: Breathe Life

The Breath is our most Simple, yet Powerful tool for Joyful Healing and Passionate Living!
Dr. Judith Kravitz

Insight 7: Stand in Your Power

I long, as does every human being, to be at home wherever I find myself.
Maya Angelou

Through the Principle of Preference you will learn to

Insight 8: Easily Allow and Receive

Deep within the essence of who we are there's a sound, a vibration, an emanation that expresses life from every cell. It resonates in harmony with all living creatures.
Dr. Barry Bittman

Insight 9: Step Into Your Brilliance

Everything in the universe has a purpose. Indeed, the invisible intelligence that flows through everything in a purposeful fashion is also flowing through you.
Wayne Dyer

Insight 10: Emphasize the Positive

One of the greatest struggles of the healing process is to forgive both yourself and others and to stop expending valuable energy on the past hurts.
Caroline Myss

Insight 11: Let Your Sun Shine

Darkness cannot drive out darkness; only light can do that. Hate cannot drive out hate; only love can do that.
Martin Luther King, Jr.

Insight 12: Apply the Art of Feeling

We create our lives by what we decide to do each day.
Bernie Siegel MD—*Mind and Heart Matters*

Insight 13: Become a Joy Catcher

Doing the best at this moment puts you in the best place for the next moment.
Oprah Winfrey

Insight 14: Love Where You're Going

What a mistake it is to assume beauty is only external.
Dr. Oz

Through the Principle of Power you will learn

Insight 15: Leading Questions to Create Your Life Your Way

As we express our gratitude, we must never forget that the highest appreciation is not to utter words, but to live by them.
John F. Kennedy

Insight 16: Make Room for Opportunity

Never look back. Concentrate on this moment forward and do everything in your power. There is no downside risk. Now you may have a chance.
Richard Bloch

Insight 17: Change It Up

You have to begin telling your story in a new way. You have to tell it as you want it to be.
Esther and Jerry Hicks
The Teachings of Abraham

Insight 18: Ask For What You Want

Sometimes people are afraid to learn just how powerful they can be.
Roxanne Useleman Hulderman

Insight 19: Reprogram Yourself Abundantly

Seeds of faith are always within us; sometimes it takes a crisis to nourish and encourage their growth.
Susan Taylor

Insight 20: Take a Goal Stroll

Cherish your visions and your dreams as they are the children of your soul, the blueprints of your ultimate achievements.
Napoleon Hill

Insight 21: Magnify Your Power

The point of power is always in the present moment.
Louise L. Hay

21 Insights to Thriving
The 3 Principles of Prosperity

Things may be a big mess in your life right now. Take heart. You have the ability to steer yourself into calmer, clearer waters. Meeting your current form of self on the road when you are distressed and freaking out can be quite the rude awakening. Not to mention how scary it is when your tried-and-true belief system proves faulty in times of real trouble. You are frustrated and overwhelmed in life. Maybe you are just plain sick and tired of your life.

You must change and you know it. Right about now, having a blueprint of what to do would be really good. You have one. You have the power to flip the script. The key here is that you recognize that you can change. All this is in your control; you are in your control. You will build trust in yourself, believe you can. The 21 Insights to Thriving Practice will help you begin to work with the 3 Principles of your Prosperity.

This practice plants the seed of your power that you will nurture its growth. It is a philosophy that centers on cultivating a positive approach in the face of adversity. The only things necessary are that you have the desire to enrich your knowledge, enlighten your experience, and be willing to try something new in a positive spirit. Somewhere along the way you just may start nodding your head yes, instead of unconsciously shaking your head no.

This practice is based on the three Principles of Prosperity: Perception, Preference, and Power. During the first seven Insights you will work with your perception. You will begin to hear and understand the story you have been telling yourself and start to flip the script. In the second seven Insights you will look to at your preference. You will begin to actively play with your choices. In the last seven Insights you will stand in your power by taking action to create your aspiration. As this practice begins to germinate and expand in your mind questions may arise. Know you are supported at www.receivebelieve.com.

To create the life you desire, you cannot continue to manifest by default. You have to give yourself directions to your destination. As you begin to create intentionally you will attract joy and abundance. You will develop balance. You will step into the flow of life by reconnecting to your true infinite supply.

The three constructs detailed in Part II are very simple and easy to use. Gently read each Insight's message. Take in what works and leave the rest. Try to read the passage again during the day. Read it when you feel stressed and want to reconnect with your power. What you take from this second reading may be more substantial than the first. Practice intentionally affirming in a daily practice. Simply say the affirmation in the morning and in the evening and intend them to be. Remember you can say the intentional affirmations and you can sing them. Let them bring you joy and assurance. Open yourself. Allow your intention's beautiful unfolding and receive it graciously.

Understanding the different components of the daily intentional affirmation:

Intentionally Affirm

I intend that _____ is mine for the asking. I now ask _____ into my life. I allow it in positively, for I know that I am safe. I am grateful, I give thanks. So be it, so it is.

The format is intentional allowing potent magnetizing of your power to attract your desired outcome. Here is the deeper meaning behind each element:

- *I intend*: you lay the path to opportunity
- *Is mine for the asking:* you acknowledge that all is possible
- *I now ask:* you ask for your blessing
- *I allow it in positively*: you allow in the high vibration
- *I know that I am safe*: soothe your subconscious fear of the unknown
- *I am grateful, I give thanks*: you appreciate the manifestation your subconscious is now designing the blueprint for.
- *So be it, so it is*: you receive as you believe

Make your intention right now for this *21 Insights to Thriving Practice.* Intend that you are more aligned with your highest vibration and magnetize your most desired aspiration. Setting your intention is a vital first step into your brilliance.

7 Insights of Improving Your Perception

During your seven Insight journey into your perception you will begin to wake up. You will take back control of your life by becoming aware of how you have been describing the facts of your life. You will reveal what truth remains in the story you have written of your life and understand if it still serves you. The filter through which you see the world is your perception. It is uniquely your own.

You become what you concentrate on. Everything you see and experience is tainted by your perception. If your perception is tinged with a steel gray of self doubt then your view into your possibilities is hampered. If you are focused on what you don't want, you will receive more of the same.

By becoming aware of your story you empower yourself to shift your perception to a more optimistic view. Begin to constructively master your inner narrator. Turn your voice to more positivity. Actively flip your script to the positive. Watch for any negativity and catch yourself. You got this, baby, it ain't no thing! If you need any additional resources, visit www.receivebelieve.com You will find valuable instruments of design to support you in your exponential growth.

I prefer to be true to myself, even at the hazard of incurring the ridicule of others, rather than to be false, and to incur my own abhorrence.
Frederick Douglass

Insight 1: Wake Up

You are reading this book likely because you have experienced a major wake up call in your life. Red Alert: you know you must do something. Your innate resources are rallying within you. Have faith in the purest of your energy. Simply know that you have been given life, therefore you have worth. Let this simple knowledge pervade you. You are worthy. Now realize that you are powered by an energy that beats your heart and pumps your blood. You have the right to call it to your aid actively. Claim your vibrant health and prosperous abundance. Your choice of what you focus on makes all the difference here in the arena of your attitude. In the end it is your attitude that wins all races.

The first step on this high road is to stop being so hard on yourself. You have done the best you could with what you had. Try to become the silent observer, the non-judgmental witness to your situation. Have compassion for yourself. Start to be with yourself profoundly by deeply embracing your inherent value. You have been born. You are here therefore you are precious. If you choose, you also have something of excellence to offer—you, fully expressed. You, actively evolving, fully vested in your life's highest good manifest. Now stop wasting time asking *Why*? Start asking *How?* Utilize whatever you've got.

Be truthful with yourself; recognize and acknowledge your shortcomings. You are defeated only when you fail to discover the truth about yourself. You cannot find the cause of your failures outside of yourself. By letting go of blame and accepting the full responsibility for your life and all its causes, you give yourself the power to create purposefully.

Bear in mind that every sense impression you receive through your five senses, influences you as surely as the sun rises in the East and sets in the West. Your mind takes in every spoken word you hear. It takes in every sight your eyes see. Your mind has unlimited capacity. Little ol' you are responsible for taking control of the programming. Be gentle with yourself as you take the helm of your focus. This is a process to be mastered. When it comes to manifesting your desired life, your thoughts should be condemned or praised for their work. How is your current thinking doing? Getting you where you want to go? If not, change.

You can begin by listening to your heart beat, simply plug your ears and listen. Think: *this primal rhythm bonds me to all living things.* You can find much comfort in the sound of your heartbeat. Listen to your heart and hear the voice of love. You are connected. You are valuable, feel it in the beating of your heart. Let it beat the resonance of your worth deeply into the fiber of your being. Meditate on your heart; look for its loving guidance. Hear your heart's song and feel what inspires you, for it is uniquely your own. Take heed and be joyous as you begin to own it. Let these miracles into your life.

Intentionally Affirm

I intend that confidence is mine for the asking. I now ask confidence into my life. I allow it in positively; for I know that I am safe. I am grateful, I give thanks. So be it, so it is.

It's not the events of our lives that shape us, but our beliefs as to what those events mean.
Tony Robbins

Insight 2: The Power of Your Story

You may well know now that experience is a teacher that shows no favorites. Her teachings are cold and unsympathetic, sometimes even brutal. Ouch, such is life. It is by progressing through pain to the positive that you truly live. Your character is built on painful times. Endure; you are a strong oak, even if today you feel like a small acorn.

You move your energy when you decide not to perceive pain in a hard fact, but instead see an opportunity to grow. Pain in life is inevitable. We all lose loved ones. Ultimately, we will all die. Suffering in life is a choice you make when you describe the pain of now or the uncertainty of your future to yourself repeatedly. Suffering and pain therefore continue to be manifest in your life. When you tell yourself the story of the pain you feel, the description you create is more than just the facts and here's where you create the gory details. No more! Intend good health and peace for yourself: *You are able to take action and face fears.*

Since birth you have been perceiving, taking in information and giving meaning to that information. You have established patterns of response to information you experienced which you refer back to when you face similar situations. This reference structure has proved itself reliable to you. You use it time and again until you now believe its results are true. Your belief system's truth is circular. It is built from your perceived experience and referenced back unto itself for validation.

You are a collection of everything you have ever distilled from your life experiences. You create adaptations to painful scenarios, like loss of love. You then design different strategies to assist you in maneuvering through your life so you experience as little pain as possible. Your subconscious programming is triggered automatically. You must intercede on your own behalf to grow past its limitations. You must reprogram yourself for higher success.

Listen to the story you are telling yourself about the cold clinical facts of your life. The facts of your life have no emotion. You give life its pain and its pleasure through your unique perception and how you interpret facts. When you get stuck in your mind, in your story, it separates you from the moment. There is only this moment. No other moment exists. You have constructed your reality through the story you tell yourself. You have a choice of perception because everything comes down to preference. What do you want in this moment?

Your mind has infinite capacity, and it is critical to realize that at all times something is always encoding your subconscious mind. Better it be you programming you. If not you, then who? Don't just let whim steal your subconscious creative power. This is very serious when you realize that your subconscious does not question the data. You, like every one of us, are constructing a map to navigate your way through life as painlessly as possible. If you do not like where you are standing then you know you need to change. Change the next thought in your mind, ask: What do I want? Shift your vibration now, you can only hold one vibration at a time, make it positive. Where there is light there is no darkness. Keep shining your light. You know the way.

Be compassionate with yourself. Look at yourself and say 'You have done the best you know how to do with the resources you had available until now.' Your belief system to this point is made up mostly of what you have been able to make up about the world and the tactics you have used to find your way through it as safely as possible.

Remember much of your belief system you constructed by default. Through environment and circumstance your young mind wrote operating programs to keep you safe. Now some of these antiquated beliefs have become negative scripts that you play out of habit. These harmful scripts prevent you from getting what you want. They muddle your preferences and keep you living in fear.

Your perception defines your life; there are no two ways about this. You can take control of your perception. Actively choose your preference in each moment. In life victory goes to those who have developed strength of character, determination and self control. Now you have options and you know it. Take an active role in your life; let your preference lead the way. Start from where you are. It is the only place you can begin.

Intentionally Affirm

I intend that choice is mine for the asking. I now ask choice into my life. I allow it in positively; for I know that I am safe. I am grateful, I give thanks. So be it, so it is.

Our thinking and our behavior are always in anticipation of a response. It is therefore fear-based.
Deepak Chopra

Insight 3: Get Aligned

Examine your thoughts, if you feel bad, blame your thoughts. When a thought comes unbidden into your mind telling you, "You are not good enough" or "You are not worth it," say to yourself ; *Aha, here I find a harmful script written by my loving younger self. This negative self talk no longer serves my highest good. It is what depresses me. I now choose a different script. I choose one that empowers me.*

You have said this disparaging thing to yourself so many times it has become your truth. Consciously grab that elusive negative impetus. This toxic thought stands between where you are and where you want to be. Know when you meet these negative thoughts in your mind that they are illusions blocking you from your aspirations. You can masterfully create your belief system to support you when you need it most. It begins with a choice, right here, right now. Choose you. You are worth it.

A primary goal of this practice is to gain control of your thoughts thereby getting a hold of your feelings. You want to start at when the negative thought first comes into your mind. Grab that negative thought and call it out as a liar and a thief. It is a liar because it is a story your perception is telling you. It is a thief because it has stolen many positive choices from you.

Remember this Law of Physics: things in motions tend to say in motion; things at rest tend to stay at rest, until acted upon by an external force. You have about 15 seconds to stop a negative thought before it becomes a full blown feeling. In a moment's choice you literally can change the direction of your life. Place in your mind, through self suggestion, the positive constructive thoughts which correspond with your greatest desire. Your mind will transform those thoughts into physical reality. Keep in mind: first came the thought, then the result. Start with your free Resource Journey at www.receivebelieve.com.

Focus your attention on controlling your thoughts. Know without a shadow of a doubt that your dominating thoughts will manifest the reality of your life. Your success or failure is defined in the nature of your thoughts. Much of your misery stems from lack of self control and self control boils down to thought control. The door to the source of your power is opened the moment you learn to control your thoughts.

Thought is the most important tool you can use to fashion your future. It is the only thing over which you have absolute control. It would be a great shame to let most of your thoughts be externally stimulated. When you deliberately choose the thoughts that dominate your mind and firmly refuse to admit outside suggestion, you are exercising the highest form of self control. You are using your free will with great proficiency.

This power of thought control is a gift given to humans. Exercise thought control well and you will be blessed with a rich life. Like attracts like. You get only what you give.

Intentionally Affirm

I intend that concentration is mine for the asking. I now ask concentration into my life. I allow it in positively; for I know that I am safe. I am grateful, I give thanks. So be it, so it is.

The roots of all goodness lie in the soil of appreciation for goodness.
Dalai Lama

Insight 4: Your Fabulous Energy

The energy that breathes you, that subtle something that animates your body, is what distinguishes life from death. Along your torso there are energy centers running life force throughout your body. It is optimal that your energy be allowed to flow freely. Right in your body you hold the key to a major contributor to your health and happiness.

By understanding how energy flows within and without your body, you gain control over the signal jams of your life. You can start directing traffic and keep your vibration humming along Divinely. Through interpreting the indicators provided by your mind, body and emotions you can steer your life in the direction you desire.

You have seven primary centers of energy, also known as chakras, which run along your upper body. Energy flows in and out of you through these energy centers. You can envision them as spinning wheels of color. It is good to understand this basic premise—your energy centers must be balanced or your life is unbalanced.

Each of the seven primary energy centers hold a life lesson on how to properly use your free will. When your focus is undisciplined, you are not allowing your energy to flow correctly throughout your body and energy blockages arise. When your energy is backed-up it leads to dis-ease. Energy gets congested through stress, stuffed emotions, negative self- talk, fear, anxiety, overwhelm, panic—the list goes on as long as you let it. Left too long dis-ease can well become a real, often dreaded, disease. It is useful to understand how to move stuck energy.

Each power center has valuable truth to share. By taking the truth into your consciousness and allowing its expression to open your experience, you shift energy. Take its truth as a lesson. Challenge your current experience. Be truthful and really discover yourself. You must start where you are. To do that you must first know where you are. Remember to be gentle with yourself. Do not judge yourself. Allow for the receipt and incorporation of the lesson from each energy center. You will be growing by leaps and bounds as an individual. Now, let's look at the layout of your super energy highway.

There are seven main energy centers along your torso that keep the energy balanced throughout your body. They are located along your body in a vertical line from the groin to the top of the head. The seven energy centers are: the root energy center, the navel energy center, the solar plexus energy center, the heart energy center, the throat energy center, the brow energy center and the crown energy center. The energy centers run up your body in the colors of the rainbow: Red, Orange, Yellow, Green, Blue, Indigo, and Violet.

Each energy center has truths to understand, lessons to learn and expressions to share.

- The root energy center is vibrant red, actively in search of safety.
- The navel energy center is bursting orange, alive with your ability to create.
- The solar plexus energy center burns yellow with your infinite power.
- The heart energy center is nurturing green, balancing your primal nature with your higher expression.
- The throat energy center is the gentle infinite blue of your truth expressed.
- The brow energy center is regal indigo, soaked with intuition and guidance.
- The crown energy center is lovely violet, connecting you to all in vibrating *I am that I am.*

If you are interested in deeper learning on how to work with your energy centers, we have a great program at www.faceforwardbook.com/tickettothrive. Each one greatly impacts your life. Each energy center has a color, a scent and offers a lesson/truth. You can focus on an unbalanced energy center and bring balance into your life. Every energy center truth has an opposite false experience, the negative. For example, if you deeply fear lack, you can work on the root lesson that you are safe. If you recognize a negative attribute in yourself, take a little time to work with balancing its corresponding energy center. You can do this easily by using the energy scent, color, sound, or by meditating its truth. The techniques are simple. They can be used in everyday life. They can provide you much needed resources which you can rely on.

Intentionally Affirm

I intend that integrity is mine for the asking. I now ask integrity into my life. I allow it in positively; for I know that I am safe. I am grateful, I give thanks. So be it, so it is.

To discover what you really believe, pay attention to the way you act— and to what you do when things don't go the way you think they should. Pay attention to what you value. Pay attention to how and on what you spend your time.
Geneen Roth

Insight 5: You Get Out What You Put In

You are suggesting to yourself all the time. When you are deeply distracted by something remember that your subconscious never stops receiving information into its programming. Every sense impression you receive through any of your five senses, influences you as surely as the sun rises in the East and sets in the West.

If you continue to suggest to yourself positively on a regular basis you will see a shift. There are many instruments of design to help you along: meditation, Qi Gong, yoga, singing, dancing, laughing, and crafts, among others. You can pivot your emotions and flip the script to the positive. If you are thinking about something negative you can ask what the opposite of it would be. You then could say: okay, I am clear on what I do not want, but what is it that I do want? Just by asking the question you are beginning to shift your vibration higher.

Keep what you do want in your line of sight. More importantly receive the possibility. Believe you can get to where you want to go. Nothing can improve until you allow it to by placing faith in yourself and opening yourself to receive. Begin to build up your chosen belief system. Start to identify with the way you want to be. Make the movie of your life the best. You are its star, its writer, and its producer, and ... ACTION! Step up your thinking, with your images, and your words to create your masterpiece. Use them consistently. Run that future reel in your mind over and over. Do not be vague with your mind. It needs you to be very specific and fantastically detailed in your future visioning. This is your story to tell. Actively engage your imagination!

Always connect the concept of safety and security with your further aspiration. No worries, in your mind make the way easy and know you will be safe when you arrive at your goal. The subconscious mind houses a deep fear of the unknown. If where you want to be has any negative associations from your past programming or the destination is new your subconscious mind will prevent you from getting there because it thinks it is not a safe place for you. Begin to allow safety into your life, say to yourself regularly: *I am safe*.

Your mind is a very complex computer. At its most basic level, it works on the concept: what goes in comes out. Nothing is changed. If you planted tomato seeds in your garden, you would not expect cabbages to grow. You attract what you focus on. For the most part, people think more about what they do not want rather than what they do want. If you continue to look for fault with your life, don't be surprised when you find it.

Your thoughts are the seeds you plant in your mind. If you are not actively tending the garden of your mind then weeds are growing, undermining your every effort. Your subconscious is a very fertile ground, please be careful what you plant. Your subconscious is most suggestible upon rising. Use some of the first 45 minutes of your day you to positively suggest to yourself. Start now, do not hesitate.

Intentionally Affirm

I intend that abundance is mine for the asking. I now ask abundance into my life. I allow it in positively; for I know that I am safe. I am grateful, I give thanks. So be it, so it is.

The Breath is our most Simple, yet Powerful tool for Joyful Healing and Passionate Living!
Dr. Judith Kravitz

Insight 6: Breathe Life

Breath aids in all things. It helps you get present quickly. There are so many ways to work with breath. Here are just a few:

- Deep diaphragmatic breathing is a great way to connect you into the moment. You can follow the breath on its journey through your body. See it entering your nose, moving down your throat into your belly, going deep in your lungs, feeding your body the stuff of life, nourishing you, healing you. Watch it leave, taking with it all your stress, toxins, disease and fear.
- Become conscious of your breath going in and out. Try to use and feel all of your lungs, from down deep in your belly up to your throat. Breathe in light and move it through your body with your breath.
- Breathe in and think, "I am calm." Breathe out and think, "I smile." Breathe with loved ones of the past and present. You can breathe with your ancestors. Meditate while you walk and mindfully breathe in for a certain number of steps and exhale for the same

amount of steps. Walk into the present moment gracefully like a lion or an elephant.

- Try the chill-out breath. Breathe out and then breathe in for a count of 5 and then breathe out for a count of six. You will find a sense of calm growing.
- Breathe out the toxins, think Darth Vader, and breathe out all the way. Get the junk out of the bottom of your lungs.
- Get centered. Try triangular breathing. Simply breathe in for a count of 4, hold for a count of 4 and breathe out for a count of 4.
- Stand in your power. Try square breathing:, just add one more side on your triangle. Breathe in for a count of 4, hold for a count of 4, breathe out for a count of 4 and hold for count of 4.
- Breathe out Fear. Breathe in through your nose, "I breathe in Peace." Breathe out through mouth, "I breathe out Fire."
- Feel safe and secure. So Hung loosely interpreted means "My identity is infinite." Breathe in through your nose "So." Breathe out through your mouth "Hung."

There is an amazing breath practice that helped me shed tons of unnecessary negative programs deep in my subconscious. It is called Transformational Breath and it really did help me to transform. It was co-created by Dr. Judith Kravitz. It is a specific breathing technique that is easily learned and wonderfully simple to use. It so positively affected my life. Transformational Breath is a great tool and best learned through an experienced breath coach. You can find a personal breath coach at www.transformationalbreathing.com. Tell them I sent you.

Intentionally Affirm

I intend that purpose is mine for the asking. I now ask purpose into my life. I allow it in positively; for I know that I am safe. I am grateful, I give thanks. So be it, so it is.

I long, as does every human being, to be at home wherever I find myself.
Maya Angelou

Insight 7: Stand in Your Power

Though life hurts sometimes, struggle is not a disadvantage. It is an advantage because it develops qualities in you that may have lain dormant without strife to awaken them. When you flip the script and perceive from a positive interpretation, you are using systems of allowing. You can move through life with minimum resistance and friction.

If you want to feel better you need to start to think differently, act differently, believe differently, and feel differently. You can do this by constantly keeping in mind precisely what you want. Your consistent focus magnetizes your point of attraction. Your emotions never lie. How you feel will tell you if your focus has been good or not. Focus on your emotions and feel your way to your future reality. Turn toward what excites you.

Your number one goal is see your glass as half full. It is the sweet sense of relief that you can reach for and win over and over. Let go of resistance. You want to change how you view and respond to life. Try to deliberately look at the positive and you will become a master framer of life.

Own your feelings and embrace them. Be okay with the fact that there will be bad shadow days. Feel free to just let it out: beat a pillow, scream, belt out a heartfelt song, take a run, punch a bag, or kick something. However, the best option of all is to have a big ol' belly laugh. Try to laugh whenever possible, especially at yourself. Laughter is one of the greatest healing agents. Studies have shown that babies laugh hundreds of times a day, but adults laugh very little. There is even a yogic practice where you just make yourself laugh. Give it a try: just laugh, pretend if you have to. You just moved energy and raised your vibration, good on you, really.

Intentionally Affirm

I intend that certainty is mine for the asking. I now ask certainty into my life. I allow it in positively; for I know that I am safe. I am grateful, I give thanks. So be it, so it is.

7 Insights of
Defining Your Preference

Your preferences guide you in this life. No one else has your unique combination of preferences. Your preferences help you discern what makes your vibration high. This creates your exceptional path in life. You have a choice of perception because everything comes down to your preferences.

Pay close attention to the areas in which you are dissatisfied. It is there you are presented with a clarifying opportunity. Through dissatisfaction you are forced to define what your preference is. By aligning your thoughts and feelings with it, you have the power to draw it to you. Take note. In life you will continually refine your preferences.

Your preference is your guide in this life. When you listen to what your heart is saying you will steer your life well. Your preference is designed choice by choice to bring you into alignment with your highest and best self. You were born therefore you have value; you have something wonderful to share. Let your preferences help you define it. When you feel excited about something you are working in the arena of your dreams.

You receive an abundance of what you ask for, get clear on what it is you want. Then ask for it and imagine its yours. Come from a place that you are enough, receive and believe it. Train your mind to seek abundance rather than lack and limitation. Look for the wonders that are present in every day life, give thanks. Appreciate, be grateful. Release resistance and welcome life's bounty.

Deep within the essence of who we are there's a sound, a vibration, an emanation that expresses life from every cell. It resonates in harmony with all living creatures.
Dr. Barry Bittman

Insight 8: Just Allow and Receive

Please believe that inherently somewhere in you there is greatness just waiting to be awakened. This is that special gift you were born to share. It is uniquely of you, for you and by you. No one can do it as well as you. You are the only person that can bring yourself peace and success. If you want more out of your life, then demand more of yourself. It is your choice whether you want to hold positive or negative habits.

By believing in this excellence in yourself, you develop the habit of self confidence which in turn opens your mind. Success is based on decisiveness and being confident will help you decide. Your biggest mission is to find the incentive that inspires you to greater action and awakens the latent giant within you. The path to this inspiring stimulus becomes apparent as you begin to focus more and more on what makes you happy and act on your preferences.

To understand the value of self reliance, sit down and become acquainted with yourself as you never have before. You can discover what strength, power and possibility lay within you. Take the time to recognize what is helping you and what is hindering you. Take action to change the harmful habits into constructive ones.

Self confidence is a product of knowledge used to inform your decision. You are condemning yourself to despair and failure; or, you are creating your triumph by the thoughts you think and thereby the feelings you feel. The best way to avail yourself of the power within you is to believe in yourself. Others will believe in you only if you believe in yourself.

Throughout your life, from birth to death, your mind is always reaching for what it does not yet possess. Therefore, ideal happiness will always be around the bend; perhaps in sight, but just out of reach. Life is never complete. No matter how much you possess there will be something else you want. The moment you cease to cherish the vision of your future you are finished. True lasting happiness is what you feel in the pursuit of an important yet unattained objective. Anticipation is life's sweetest elixir.

Preferentially point your focus. You will resemble, tomorrow, the dominating thoughts of your mind today. Plant a seed for tomorrow wisely. Frame life in your mind nicely, by seeking and speaking of the good. You have constructed your reality through the story you tell yourself. *So start telling yourself a better story.*

Start filtering out negative scripts that no longer serve your highest good. When it comes to manifesting, your thoughts should be condemned or praised for their work. Focus on your emotions and feel your way to your future reality. Choice by choice, reach for relief and let go of resistance. Let your preference be your guide. You want to change how you view and respond to life. Have your own back. Deliberately look at the positive. You will become the master framer of your life.

You are human. You are going to have good and bad times. When you are down, bear in mind that it is all about how quickly you rebound that counts. You can get rid of low frequencies in your life by adding high frequencies. You can start with supplementing your life with whatever gets you feeling good.

Lack of faith is the killer of dreams. Lack of faith usually displays itself through worry, anxiety and frustration. Just be assured that whatever you want to create in this life, you can. Choose to be confident enough to just take action. Base your actions in Can-Do faith. Don't be one of the many who are mentally on crutches because they do not believe enough in themselves.

Intentionally Affirm

I intend that grace is mine for the asking. I now ask grace into my life. I allow it in positively for I know that I am safe. I am grateful, I give thanks. So be it, so it is.

Everything in the universe has a purpose. Indeed, the invisible intelligence that flows through everything in a purposeful fashion is also flowing through you.
Wayne Dyer

Insight 9: Step into Your Brilliance

Plato's Law of Affinity states like attracts like. What you are thinking creates a feeling. This feeling creates your point of attraction. This point of attraction will draw like vibrations.

Your actions will always reflect your dominating thoughts. Singleness of purpose is essential for success. Your enthusiasm is a vital force that impels action. Mix enthusiasm into your everyday activities to stay energized. When you deliberately choose the thoughts that dominate your mind, and firmly refuse to admit outside suggestion, you are exercising the highest form of self control.

Be aware of how each thought feels. Use your focus to expand your possibilities. Improve your point of attraction by choosing to focus on good vibrations. Your primary power in this life is the point of your focus. Your focus point is how you interpret this life, how you tell yourself your story. The opportunity is on and it's all up to you. You control your focus. You're in the driver's seat. You can decide where to direct your life.

Your life is really your preferences. Start using your power of choice. Add choice points throughout the day. Whenever you feel stressed or catch yourself running a negative tape, you can now pause and realize you have the power to choose a better now.

You may get depressed but know that you have the power to decide. You can focus your thoughts positively and send better messages to your body. Whatever happens, you can handle it. Learn to trust that everything you need will be there when you need it. Your mind is a powerful healer. You can visualize healing occurring within you, anytime. You are in charge. You know what is best for you. You are responsible for satisfying your own needs.

Feeling creates a point of attraction, calling like to like. The key to feeling powerful is to understand how the thoughts you are focusing on create your feelings. Thoughts become feelings in about 15 seconds. If your thoughts are not taking you in good direction, stop them.

Life is a continuous to-do list. You will never get it all done, so give yourself a break. Be truly you, for you. Say yes when you mean yes and no when you mean no. Stop selling your time cheaply. Buy back your self-worth. Take the time you need. Take ownership of your present.

When you feel good, realize it and get to know the cause. You can then use that cause for a positive effect often. The best of life is the birth of desire. Focus on what enlivens your life.

Now is the best time; for there is no other moment but this one right now. It is foolish to look to the past for better times. Understand that life is never complete. It is not your job to try to complete it. So take a breather and let yourself be okay right now in this moment. STOP. You okay?

Intentionally Affirm

I intend that desire is mine for the asking. I now ask desire into my life. I allow it in positively; for I know that I am safe. I am grateful, I give thanks. So be it, so it is.

One of the greatest struggles of the healing process is to forgive both yourself and others and to stop expending valuable energy on the past hurts.
Caroline Myss

Insight 10: Emphasize the Positive

Consider that it is said, the better part of success is just showing up. You can find success by living your life made by your own choices. You are now empowered to change the patterns of behavior that no longer serve you. You can look at each one of your beliefs and rebuild your belief system to suit your aspirations in life.

Today is a new day. Decide to take your life in hand and succeed. Just flip your script. You are the creator of your life's story after all. Your potential is unlimited. Be a problem solver look for solutions. You may not be able to control your circumstances but you can control your thoughts.

Open your heart and believe in the possibilities of you. Think about your positive qualities and they will grow. This is a secret of happiness. Accept that you have to continually improve your ways of thinking and feeling. When you feel bad, reach for a good notion and choose to feel better. Make the direction of your next thought positive. Look to your preference, it will lead you straight. You can shift your consciousness from one feeling to another. It is your choice what you decide to emphasize. Focus on what you want.

Make it a practice to wake up first thing in the morning and think of all the positive things that can happen that day. Find happiness in who you are and what you have, here and now. Stand in your power. Ask yourself frequently, "What is good in my life? What can I be happy about?" You will soon find that you have a lot to be grateful for. Instead of asking what's wrong; ask what's right.

To improve the quality of your experience you can't let your circumstances dictate how you feel. You can feel the feelings you want on a consistent basis. Your state of being equals your thoughts and feelings. Your thoughts and feelings should serve you. If they no longer serve you then change them. Your perception, this filter you see the world through, affects how you feel. Attempt to interpret things the best way you can moment to moment.

Negative beliefs like: "I am not enough," "I may fail," and "People will laugh," only hold you back from your true potential. Attitude is everything. Make your attitude serve you. How you look at the world dictates your attitude. Your attitude creates your circumstances. It is not what happens to you but how you interpret life that counts.

Intentionally Affirm

I intend that self love is mine for the asking. I now ask self love into my life. I allow it in positively, for I know that I am safe. I am grateful, I give thanks. So be it, so it is.

Darkness cannot drive out darkness; only light can do that. Hate cannot drive out hate; only love can do that.
Martin Luther King, Jr.

Insight 11: Let Your Sun Shine

Weight the scales of your day more positively. Give yourself more choices and begin to make better decisions. You are putting mechanisms in place to shield yourself from negative influences and self-defeating patterns. You can begin to use suggestion to influence your life just by focusing on the good stuff. Simply, think of what you want instead of what you don't. You can take your life where you want it to go. Get psyched.

Let's do the math: 24 hours make up 100% of your day. Imagine two scales counter balancing each other, one side positive and the other negative, measuring the use of your time. Your goal is to tip the scales of time to the positive, but you don't want to just tip them, you want to slam dunk it. If you make the last thought before sleep a good one, you will reprogram your subconscious mind positively during sleep. You will begin your day 33% positive. Thought by thought, decision by decision, action by action, you will tilt the percentages of fortune in your favor. You are updating your belief system.

Begin to add choice to your daily routine and play with your options. Have some fun going with your unique preference. Let yourself feel free to decide. As you stay more positive each day, your desires will stir. Your enthusiasm will gain momentum. New horizons open up as you follow your interests to discover what you desire most in life. The process is simple: in the moment ask, "What is my preference here? What would my heart say? Which feels better?" Then trust, decide and act. Everyday will be an opportunity to enhance your state of mind.

Your purposeful passion will become defined, preference by preference, glittering on the horizon, beckoning you forward. You now have a destination in life, a map to gain your bearings whenever you feel lost. As you start to name your desire, intend to devote time daily to acquiring it. An insightful shortcut to your desired goal is learning about who you most admire and understanding why.

One wonderful way to really feel amazing is to close your eyes and think of the blazing sun. See the sun shining brightly, blinding with its intensity. Then, allow in your mind's eye your energy to merge with that of the sun. Become one with the sun, feel the power seeping into all that you are, filling you up with pure light. Get your fill of the power, plug in. Shine down on all you love. See them raise their heads to take in your brilliant light and warmth.

The following are some additional ways you can feel more optimistic and thereby attract more positivity to you:

healthy eating	reading
physical exercise	singing
meditation	dancing
intentional affirmations	looking at a flower feeling the sun
personal practice	on your face
helping someone complimenting/	listening to the ocean
encouraging yourself or others	gazing at the stars
laughing	visualizing success
smiling	feeling joyful
learning	feeling enthusiastic
saying "I love you" to yourself	good conversation
and others	a hug
saving money	being in nature
being aware of your breath	skipping

The list goes on and on.

Fill your days creating. Let your story today be what you want. Focus on things that make you feel good. Find success by living your life made from your own choices. Become the creator of your life's story, rewrite it.

Just try to make the highest and best choice in every moment you can. You will know it by how good you feel. Love is the highest and best of life. Its vibration is the highest you can offer.

Intentionally Affirm

I intend that happiness is mine for the asking. I now ask happiness into my life. I allow it in positively; for I know that I am safe. I am grateful, I give thanks. So be it, so it is.

We create our lives by what we decide to do each day.
Bernie Siegel MD—*Mind and Heart Matters*

Insight 12: The Art of Feeling

You can literally feel your way to prosperity. Use your emotions as your guide. Pay close attention to your emotions. The better you feel the more in harmony you are with attaining your desire. When you allow, you are aligned with flow of life. When you resist, you are doing just that, resisting life's offerings.

Begin to be alert to how you feel when you think about different things and how environments and people trigger your reactions. Become aware of how your automatic thoughts make you feel. Are your thoughts taking you toward or away from what you desire? The better you feel, the closer you are moving toward your goal.

Although thoughts can just seem to pop into your head, you are responsible for their direction. Your control starts with your awareness of how you feel in response to that automatic thought. Then moving your focus in a better direction starting with your next thought, make it feel better. Become aware of how each thought feels. Use your focus to expand your possibilities. Improve your point of attraction by choosing to focus on good vibrations, like love.

When you think a thought over and over again, it becomes easier and easier to refer to that thought again. When you think about something for more than a quarter of a minute, you attach an emotion to that thought. The thought becomes emotional. Your emotions are powerful attractors. The thought which is now an emotion is compounded as that emotion becomes a point of attraction. Dominant thoughts become deeply emotional beliefs attracting like vibrations consistently enough to create physical evidence. Now your thought has become your truth. You feel vindicated as you can then point to physical proof positive that your belief was correct. It's time to break the cycle.

In the moment-to-moment of your life, reach for relief. When you feel relief you have won in that very moment. Feel better by reaching for relief by thinking better feeling thoughts. Do this consistently enough and you will see that which you truly want become your reality. Bridging the "here of dissatisfaction" to the "there of accomplishment" is where the interesting stuff of life happens. The creative way you design the path to bridge the difference from where you are and where you want to be is the playful arena of a life well lived.

Focus on your emotions and feel your way to your future reality. Choice-by-choice, reach for relief and let go of resistance. You want to change how you view and respond to life. Be deliberate. Look for the positive and you will become the master framer of your life.

You have the power to set yourself up for a better day at any time. When you are about to start something new, take a moment and see it go the way you want. Set yourself up so that what comes next is good for you. Now you've got your back.

Grow your power by directing your thoughts to the positive. Allow yourself to be positively playful. You have the ability to put your life in a sweet frame, designed exactly to your liking. You can have faith that the best is yet to come.

The more you think a thought, the easier it becomes to defer to it. So start training your mind to think positively. Align your thoughts to feeling better. Stay alert for points of resistance: in the form of stress, worry, anger, and sadness. Turn your focus to see the positive possibilities. Feel better by active choice. Your power lies in your point of focus. What are you paying attention to?

Intentionally Affirm

I intend that love is mine for the asking. I now ask love into my life. I allow it in positively; for I know that I am safe. I am grateful, I give thanks. So be it, so it is.

Doing the best at this moment puts you in the best place for the next moment.
Oprah Winfrey

Insight 13: Become a Joy Catcher

Joy catchers are a wonderful way to add pleasure and appreciation to your days. Life is so busy and sometimes you have too much on your plate. When it all seems like a big pain, it is great to have the tools to turn things around. Using a joy catcher can give you the power to have more good days than bad. You can be more gratefully alive.

When you find yourself totally enchanted by one of life's many wonders, take a moment to attach yourself to the moment. Feel how it feels to be in love with the present. Allow yourself to be delighted to live in the world. Attach some motion that is unique to you. Use something that can be re-used under any number of circumstances. You can snap your fingers or clap your hands, jump, smile, sing, touch your ring. The movement, word, or touch has the power to bring you back to that moment whenever you want to feel better. There are so many ways to say I love you to yourself. It's an easy way to help yourself feel better.

Songs have a way of moving you to a state of exultation and celebration. These are some high vibrations. There is such a beauty to singing it out. Songs can bring you to states of powerful self expression. Use this power frequently; free yourself through song any time you feel like it. Sing songs from your heart or sing songs that you know. Have a song in your back pocket for a rainy day. You can rely on song to help you through your days.

Scenic vistas are full of pleasure and beauty. You can recall them or inhale them. Think of a field of sun flowers, all open and shining in the sun, swaying gently in the breeze. Envision a baby laughing, feel that giddy joy burgeoning in your chest. Have a bunch of scenes that you can pull up on a whim and flip through on the movie screen of your mind. You can include a beautiful sunset over the ocean, a rainbow in the sky after the rain, the sky all misty and dusted with color, add your own personal favorites.

Intentionally Affirm

I intend that pleasure is mine for the asking. I now ask pleasure into my life. I allow it in positively; for I know that I am safe. I am grateful, I give thanks. So be it, so it is.

What a mistake it is to assume beauty is only external.
Dr. Oz

Insight 14: Love Where You're Going

At all times, you are both disseminating and receiving vibrations. The vibration you emit is based primarily in your feelings. Your subconscious mind is like a magnet. When it is vitalized and energized with fervent intentions, it attracts all that is necessary to fulfill your dreams.

Your goals in life need to be backed by passion for their attainment. Your preference is the factor which determines what your purpose in life will be. No one can select what you desire but yourself. Select your principal aspiration with care. Let it be one that will bring you happiness, peace and prosperity that endures. After you have selected it, write it out. Place it where you will see it at least once a day. You have to start where you are. If you have no clue what you want, start with anything that comes to mind and refine that a little every day until it feels right for you. The psychosomatic effect of seeing it regularly impresses this purpose in your subconscious mind so strongly that it accepts it and begins to create it.

This subconscious blueprint sets your preferences and will eventually lead your activities in life and direct you, step-by-step, toward the attainment of the object of your ambition. Suggest to yourself repeatedly that you will attain your goal. Visit www.receivebelieve.com for a free Resource Journey to help you enthusiastically visualize your success regularly. Have the resolve to hold this success image in your mind with full faith until it influences you to take the necessary steps to attain it. Think of your success before you go to sleep: imagine yourself meeting with top advisors on your victory strategy. Allow yourself to receive their wisdom.

Until you select a primary ambition in life, you dissipate your energies. This leaves you feeling weak and indecisive. When you organize your focus and direct your faculties toward the attainment of a definite purpose, you take advantage of developing the power of organized effort. Organized effort is a means of attaining the necessary power with which to materialize your objective. By constantly keeping in mind precisely what you want, your point of attraction becomes like a magnifying glass under direct sun, able to start a fire. Once the habit of working with a primary goal is instilled, you will become a person of prompt and definite decisions. Concentration of effort and working with a chief aim are two essential factors in success.

Keep an open mind. Skepticism is the foe of self development. Fear is the main reason for unhappiness and despair. Many times it can immobilize you. Fear keeps many people as only spectators in the back row of life because they are too busy wondering, "What will they say?" Mastering the fear that whispers in your ear, "You cannot do it," is the key to your happiness. Be a player in the game of life. Step courageously onto the playing field.

Intentionally Affirm

I intend that power is mine for the asking. I now ask power into my life. I allow it in positively; for I know that I am safe. I am grateful, I give thanks. So be it, so it is.

7 Insights to
Controlling Your Power

When you begin to actually apply your power by taking action, you move energy. When you move energy, you create change. You are blessed with free will which you can consciously use to design the life you desire. You are only limited by your own doubts. When you focus your attention on what you want in life, the opportunities are endless.

A belief is simply a thought you have over and over. You have the ability to change your beliefs. You can simply think a more positive thought over and over, thereby instilling a new and improved belief. When you believe in yourself, then anything is possible. Your belief will grow as you decide and act consistently based on your preference. Your preference becomes clearer with use and grows as you focus on what you want.

To stop suffering you must change your negative thought patterns. When you face difficult times, look at them as opportunities to get clear on what you really want. You can be deliberately attractive in your life. When you take back your focus you put the power back into your life. You can choose to deliberately create the life of your dreams. Focus your thoughts to stand in your power and step into your brilliance.

As we express our gratitude, we must never forget that the highest appreciation is not to utter words, but to live by them.
John F. Kennedy

Insight 15: Leading Questions to Create Your Life Your Way

You have a problem-solving mind. It will endeavor to solve any problem you throw its way. Use your amazing power to ask better questions. Every thought begins with a question, so why not control the process? You can start to lead your mind to solve your life's problems with Leading Questions. It is good to get into the habit of asking them every day. You can ask Leading Questions any time. Ask them sets of three. Center your questions around good vibrations like: vibrant health, success, love, kindness, abundance, joy, strength, or connection.

3 Power Questions:
How can I…?
What will I do that…?
Wouldn't it be nice if…?

Example:

How can I be happy today?
What will I do that I am happy today?
Wouldn't it be great if I am happy today?

Ask powerful questions of your problem solving mind to lead you to your aspiration.

* By asking "How can I…?" you engage your mind to provide you with tangible steps.
* Through inquiring "What will I do that…?" Your mind will look to provide concrete answers to yield your sought after result.
* Request your mind to imagine by asking "Wouldn't it be great if…?" Give your subconscious something constructive to work on.

Ask your limitless mind all your questions, and then trust in faith, not fear. Open your heart. Believe in the possibilities of you. Be optimistic in that infinite energy that beats your heart. Only lack of confidence will obstruct you. Have wonderful dreams and believe they will come true.

You will always find what you are looking for whether it is good or bad. Seek the good. Think about your positive qualities and they will grow. Accept that you have to continually improve your way of thinking and feeling. Remember to ask for what you need, just ask for it with happy expectancy.

Intentionally Affirm

I intend that trust is mine for the asking. I now ask trust into my life. I allow it in positively; for I know that I am safe. I am grateful, I give thanks. So be it, so it is.

Never look back. Concentrate on this moment forward and do everything in your power. There is no downside risk. Now you may have a chance.
Richard Bloch

Insight 16: Make Room for Opportunity

Opportunity may be found wherever you really look for it. To be able to capitalize on opportunity when it arises, you must have some cash reserves. To build a cash reserve, you must save a portion of your income. As you learn to pay yourself first, your perceived value will increase.

Forming the habit of saving in a systematic manner, places in you in the way of greater opportunity. It gives you vision, self confidence, and enthusiasm to increase your earning capacity. This practice will destroy your poverty-consciousness. Having savings sets up a prosperity-consciousness. You begin to demand prosperity and expect it. You have prepared yourself to receive it and use it wisely. Form the habit of thinking and talking of prosperity and abundance. Soon material evidence will manifest in the nature of wider, opportunity, both new and unexpected.

Without savings you suffer in two ways: first, by the inability to seize opportunities that come only to the person with some ready cash, and second, by embarrassment due to lack of reserve capital for emergencies. Most of us have developed the Habit of Spending while neglecting the Habit of Saving. The Habit of Saving requires self-control and self-sacrifice, in other words, more force of character than most of us have developed. Over time the Habit of Saving also gives a thrill that spending cannot, as more and more opportunity is seized.

The rule is that if you follow the systematic Habit of Saving, a definite proportion of all the money you earn and receive, you are certain to place yourself in a position of financial independence. If you save nothing, you can be sure you will never be financially independent, no matter how great your income.

Intentionally Affirm

I intend that opportunity is mine for the asking. I now ask opportunity into my life. I allow it in positively; for I know that I am safe. I am grateful, I give thanks. So be it, so it is.

You have to begin telling your story in a new way. You have to tell it as you want it to be.
Esther and Jerry Hicks
The Teachings of Abraham

Insight 17: Change It Up

Your subconscious mind wants to feel safe and generally steers clear of the unknown. It would rather replay a negative habit even though it is painful instead of experiencing something new. Your ego is your personal defense system that warns you of danger. It is its job to find things for you be afraid of. The Ego's story is one based in fear. Attach safety to your desired destination and move quickly through fear into action and progress. Trust that everything you need will be there when you need it.

From the familiarity that a habit breeds, a false sense of safety develops. Your subconscious is programmed to seek safety. When a habit is well formed, the subconscious mind affixes itself to the well-trodden course of your habit. Any habit can be discontinued by building in its place a more desirable habit.

Nature hates a void. It will fall back into the last habit just to keep the void filled. The only way to break a bad habit is to replace it with a desirable habit. Every time you travel over the path of your new desirable habit, that path becomes easier to travel in the future. Practice becoming a good path maker. Carve your path as clear and deep as you can at the beginning so that you can readily see it the next time you wish to follow it.

To form a new habit, visualize your success; feel good about it. Put force and enthusiasm into the new experience and blaze that path. Forget all about the old paths; concern yourself with only the new ones that you are building to your specifications. Travel over your newly-made paths as often as possible. The more often you go over the new paths, the sooner they will become worn and easily traveled.

Habit is the pivotal point on which accomplishment turns. Intend that you acquire the habits that lead you to move through life with an abundance of health, unfaltering faith, unceasing energy, endless optimism and boundless confidence.

Intentionally Affirm

I intend that persistence is mine for the asking. I now ask persistence into my life. I allow it in positively; for I know that I am safe. I am grateful, I give thanks. So be it, so it is.

Sometimes people are afraid to learn just how powerful they can be.
Roxanne Usleman Hulderman

Insight 18: Ask For What You Want

You must ASK for help; just simply ask for it. Now have faith that solutions will come. You can increase your asking power by asking while holding your left hand cupped, palm up. Ask and intend that all you need is being received by you right now. Say thank you, vibrate appreciation. Ask to release the fear and to help you have courage. Allow yourself to feel safe and to easily receive more and more of life's abundant offering.

There are so many wonderful ways to invite in the help you need. Your asking is a very personal and private ritual. Find a way that you can use to comfortably and consistently request what you need. Summon it, invoke it, and pray for it: then, prepare to be blessed with the solution to your problem. Ask for a meeting with the Highest Council before you sleep to have all your issues strategically maneuvered. You can just offer up your problems, then trust the solutions will come to you as you need them. Roxanne Hulderman guides you to ask your angels for help. Ask them three times and don't forget to say thank you. Ask your Source, your Highest Good to aide you. Call power to you. It is yours in the form you can accept. Ask, expect, and allow the receipt of your desires.

To truly live authentically you must stand in your power. You must know that you are enough. Affirmations are a positive statement you say about yourself. An example of an affirmation is: I am healthy and vibrant.

A good affirmation needs to be personal, positive, in present tense, and emotionalized by being stated aloud with passion. By adding intention you compound the power of affirmations and create synergy.

Try this simple statement:
        I intend that I am (say something positive).

For example:

I intend that I am always protected.
I intend that I am sheltered by love.
I intend that I am well.
I intend that I am joyful.

Intentionally Affirm

I intend that security is mine for the asking. I now ask security into my life. I allow it in positively; for I know that I am safe. I am grateful, I give thanks. So be it, so it is.

Seeds of faith are always within us; sometimes it takes a crisis to nourish and encourage their growth.
Susan Taylor

Insight 19: Reprogram Yourself Abundantly

You are now reprogramming, recording over all the old messages that do not work for you anymore. You are building new successful messages. Know that it is okay to have some "oh well" days. You are not trying to be perfect here. Do not beat yourself up. Just get up, dust yourself off and continue feeling forward positively.

Most of your negative behaviors are in your subconscious mind. You would not consciously sabotage yourself. You need to work with reprogramming the subconscious mind. Suggestion is a tool of the subconscious mind.

Your mind is made up of two parts, the conscious and the subconscious. The conscious mind houses your will power, your analytical skills, and your reasoning. This equals only about one quarter of your mind. The subconscious mind makes up the majority of your mind, it is where imagination and all your beliefs are stored. Your subconscious also houses your body's operating system. It was in early childhood that you gathered the beliefs that formed your own unique belief system.

Suggestion asks you to just engage that imagination of yours. Go with it; allow your suggestibility. Relax and accept the story of your visualization. Like when you are reading a good book and you get wrapped up in the plot, give yourself over to the feelings created by your imaginings.

If you are living defensively, you wake up every morning and go about life with beliefs that you happened to pick up along the way. You can now start to live offensively, and ask, "Does this belief actually still work for me?" If it does not, you can shift that belief to something that serves you.

The best of life is in the now and the possibilities of a masterfully created future. To name your desire start looking for that giddy feeling of excitement; you know, like a kid in a candy store. When you feel anticipation rush in, you know you are on to the thread of your aspiration. The process of manifesting is based on your emotions. Your emotions create vibrations that draw like vibrations, so get excited about what you want.

There is no greater feeling than a desire burgeoning in your breast and coming plainly to the front of your mind. This is your driving force. From this point onward look for and enjoy the birth of your new desires. Your desire enlivens your life; it leads you to your fulfillment enthusiastically. Desires have strong summoning power in the Law of Affinity. When you are enthused by a desire, you are effectively magnetizing and summoning it to you. The more excitement you feel the more draw it has. The more time you spend believing it, the closer you pull it to you.

When you are energized and feeling good, recognize it and take a moment to understand what it is that you are enjoying. This is what energizes you. When you find yourself so pleasurably involved with something that you lose track of time, remember it and please repeat, repeat, repeat it. Aim to feel good and make it happen by active choice.

Intentionally Affirm

I intend that enthusiasm is mine for the asking. I now ask enthusiasm into my life. I allow it in positively; for I know that I am safe. I am grateful, I give thanks. So be it, so it is.

Cherish your visions and your dreams as they are the children of your soul, the blueprints of your ultimate achievements.
Napoleon Hill

Insight 20: Take a Resource Journey

Your subconscious mind can be controlled and directed by your conscious (voluntary) mind. Any idea or thought which is held in the mind, through repetition, has a tendency to direct the physical body to transform such thought or idea into its material equivalent.

The subconscious mind accepts and acts upon all information that reaches it, whether constructive or destructive. It does not matter where the information comes from, within your conscious mind or outside of it. In this, as in many things, concentration is the key to success. Stimulate your mind with a strong, deeply-seated desire so that the powers of your mind will function constructively. Desire is the seed of all achievement.

Your imagination is the most amazing gift. First your imagination forms your thoughts, then it organizes the thought into ideas and plans, then you see the evidence of the transformation of those plans into reality. Let your goals become truth in your imagination first. Fully vest into acknowledging your attainment of your ideal. In other words, Receive it and then Believe it.

The process of manifesting is based on your emotions. Your emotions create vibrations that draw like vibrations. The way you create is through your feelings. Feelings create strong vibrations and like attracts like. Figure out what you truly hunger for; and get really clear on it. Subsequently, you can start a practice of "Resource Journeys." To help your desires manifest first you need to know what you want, then get into a high frequency and go on a "Resource Journey."

To Resource Journey most effectively first get into a high vibration. Some easy ways to raise your frequency are to rent a comedy, start laughing, or you can sing, or dance. There is a Tibetan practice that you turn 21 times in a circle, clock wise, to raise your vibration. You can also practice vibrating energy up your body by shaking your body as if you had violent shivers. Another practice that can raise your vibration is to cover your right eye, look into mirror, breathe in "Hung" and breathe out "Sa," in about a minute you can feel your energy shift.

Once you know what your aspiration is take a "Resource Journey" and see yourself attaining your goal. The more you visualize living your dream, the more real you can make it. The more precise your vision is the better. When you are On a Resource Journey or practicing Intentional Affirmations do it with great feeling, really receive your upcoming good with certainty. The more deeply you feel your future reality, the more powerfully you draw it to you. Involve sound in your visualization. Make up a script with anything you would hear if your dream was coming true, hear yourself telling your friends and loved ones of your fantastic successes. Resonate in this high vibration and be grateful.

When you want something take a minute and go on a "Resource Journey" whenever you are in a high frequency throughout your day. Know you are actively creating a powerfully positive point of attraction. Congratulate yourself; you are becoming the true artisan of your life.

Intentionally Affirm

I intend that energy is mine for the asking. I now ask energy into my life. I allow it in positively; for I know that I am safe. I am grateful, I give thanks. So be it, so it is.

The point of power is always in the present moment.
Louise L. Hay

Insight 21: Magnify Your Power

Every second of every day you are making choices; this is the basis of free will. To be deliberately attractive you must direct your thoughts. Life can be a process of conscious choices rather than a series of defensive reactions. The present moment is pregnant with possibilities. It is your assignment, should you chose to accept it, to find yourself positively present, as in here now. However, this is not mission impossible, but **mission possible**. Notice you always have the choice of what you focus on.

The faculties of your mind can shrivel and waste away from neglect. Self-confidence is no exception, it is developed by use or it fades. Inaction leads to atrophy. Ambition and self-confidence are indispensable qualities to battle complacency. Struggle is not a disadvantage. It is an advantage that develops character in you. Your greatness may have lain dormant if not awakened by strife. Being forced by circumstance to do your best breeds restraint, self-control, and commitment to change. By overcoming struggle you become persistent. Persistence is a most valuable ally.

Self-confidence is infectious. It is impelling. It persuades. It draws others and the results you seek. Self-confidence starts from enthusiasm. When you are enthused about something, pay attention; your aspiration lies down that path.

Grow your power by directing your thoughts to the positive perspective. Offer up your problems and see each being solved. You can invite your higher self to direct your life and then step graciously out of your own way. Have faith.

A better feeling is a moment's choice away. Reach for relief.

- Dream work: write questions and put them under your pillow before sleeping. Trust the answer will come.
- Automatic writing: ask your question and just start writing whatever comes to you.
- Candles soothes: stare into a flame and see the ever changing beauty of life.
- Flower appreciation: study a flower, really look into it, and see its infinite beauty.
- Feel some Good Vibrations: be light hearted, laugh, smile, give comfort, hope, be joyful, feel certainty.

Intentionally Affirm

I intend that ease is mine for the asking. I now ask ease into my life. I allow it in positively; for I know that I am safe. I am grateful, I give thanks. So be it, so it is.

Let us Support You in Opening the Door to Your Possibilities

You are so valuable and we just want to make sure you know it. Permit us to assist you to live your life to its highest and best. Please come and visit us and receive free insights and tips to help you power your life.

The 21 Insights to Thriving is a door to your brilliance. To become a master in your life you will need to make your practice a joy. As a gift for visiting our community at www.receivebelieve.com/tickettothrive, you will receive a complimentary Ticket to Thrive including solid tactical resources to help you gather your confidence and take action for your own benefit.

If you are reading this, you understand you have what it takes to move forward and reclaim your life. Receive Believe stands ready to support you so you can emerge glorious in your new found power. You are going to emerge better from having weathered this troubled time. We want you thriving living a life full of joy, freedom and growth. Receive Believe is all about making your smile grow. Our desire is to assist you to stand in your power, step into your brilliance and masterfully create your life.

Receive Believe is all about flipping the script on your shattering life event. This scary thing can empower you. Receive Believe is dedicated to offering you a comprehensive approach to maximum well-being during this challenging time and beyond. This philosophy centers on cultivating a positive approach in the face of adversity. You are brave and committed to yourself and should be congratulated. You are investing time and money on improving yourself. Statistically speaking this is just plain smart of you.

Desire is at the heart of all achievement. As you intentionally awaken your passion, you enrich your life. Our goal is to help you feel more positive each day. While you build positive power, it outweighs negative patterns and you begin to receive wins. With each win your belief in your possibilities solidifies and becomes the foundation on which to build your dreams. We will assist you in making crisis a chance for life transformation. So let's get you started Receiving and Believing, join us at www.receivebelieve.com/tickettothrive.

Allow us to give you the means to start with the end in mind.

Visit today – www.receivebelieve.com/tickettothrive

BUY A SHARE OF THE FUTURE IN YOUR COMMUNITY

These certificates make great holiday, graduation and birthday gifts that can be personalized with the recipient's name. The cost of one S.H.A.R.E. or one square foot is $54.17. The personalized certificate is suitable for framing and will state the number of shares purchased and the amount of each share, as well as the recipient's name. The home that you participate in "building" will last for many years and will continue to grow in value.

Here is a sample SHARE certificate:

THIS CERTIFIES THAT
YOUR NAME HERE
HAS INVESTED IN A HOME FOR A DESERVING FAMILY

1985-2010
TWENTY-FIVE YEARS OF BUILDING FUTURES
IN OUR COMMUNITY ONE HOME AT A TIME

1200 SQUARE FOOT HOUSE @ $65,000 = $54.17 PER SQUARE FOOT
This certificate represents a tax deductible donation. It has no cash value.

YES, I WOULD LIKE TO HELP!

*I support the work that Habitat for Humanity does and I want to be part of the excitement! As a donor, I will receive periodic updates on your construction activities but, more importantly, I know my gift will help a family in our community realize the dream of homeownership. **I would like to SHARE in your efforts against substandard housing in my community!** (Please print below)*

PLEASE SEND ME _____ SHARES at $54.17 EACH = $ $_____

In Honor Of: _____

Occasion: (Circle One)   HOLIDAY   BIRTHDAY   ANNIVERSARY

       OTHER: _____

Address of Recipient: _____

Gift From: _____ *Donor Address:* _____

Donor Email: _____

I AM ENCLOSING A CHECK FOR $ $_____ PAYABLE TO HABITAT FOR HUMANITY <u>OR</u> PLEASE CHARGE MY VISA OR MASTERCARD *(CIRCLE ONE)*

Card Number _____ Expiration Date: _____

Name as it appears on Credit Card _____ Charge Amount $ _____

Signature _____

Billing Address _____

Telephone # Day _____ Eve _____

PLEASE NOTE: Your contribution is tax-deductible to the fullest extent allowed by law.
Habitat for Humanity • P.O. Box 1443 • Newport News, VA 23601 • 757-596-5553
www.HelpHabitatforHumanity.org

CPSIA information can be obtained
at www.ICGtesting.com
Printed in the USA
FFOW05n0749190914